Military-to-Civilian

CAREER TRANSITION GUIDE

The Essential Job Search Handbook for Service Members

jist®
Works
America's Career Publisher

Janet I. Farley

Military-to-Civilian Career Transition Guide

© 2005 by Janet I. Farley

Published by JIST Works, an imprint of JIST Publishing, Inc.
8902 Otis Avenue
Indianapolis, IN 46216-1033
Phone: 1-800-648-JIST   Fax: 1-800-JIST-FAX   E-mail: info@jist.com

Visit our Web site at **www.jist.com** for information on JIST, free job search tips, book chapters, and ordering instructions for our many products! For free information on 14,000 job titles, visit www.careeroink.com.

See the back of this book for additional JIST titles and ordering information. Quantity discounts are available for JIST books. Please call our Sales Department at 1-800-648-5478 for a free catalog and more information.

Acquisitions Editor: Lori Cates Hand
Development Editor: Michael Thomas
Interior Designers: designLab, Seattle
Page Layout: Deb Kincaid
Cover Designer: Nick Anderson
Proofreader: Linda Quigley
Indexer: Tina Trettin

Printed in Canada.
08 07 06 05 04   9 8 7 6 5 4 3 2 1

Library of Congress Cataloging-in-Publication Data

Farley, Janet I.
  Military-to-civilian career transition guide : the essential
job search handbook for service members / Janet I. Farley.
     p. cm.
  Includes index.
  ISBN 1-59357-091-0
  1. Career changes—United States. 2. Job hunting—United States. 3.
  Retired military personnel—Employment—United States. 4.
  Veterans—Employment—United States. I. Title.
  HF5384.F37 2005
  650.14—dc22
                           2004015097

ISBN 1-59357-091-0

CONTENTS

Chapter 1: Should You Stay or Should You Go?   **1**

Considering All Your Options   2

When You Don't Have a Choice
in the Matter   2

What to Know Before You Make It Public
Knowledge   3

The Hardest Thing About Leaving
the Military   4

Anticipating the Culture Shock   6

**Chapter 2: Creating Your Overall Transition
Strategy**   **9**

Your End Game and Transition Timeline   9

The Ever-Burning Question Remains:
What Do You Do When in the
Transition Process?   10

Military Transition Assistance   27

Visiting the Transition Assistance Office   27

Your Preseparation Counseling Checklist   29

Stress   32

Employment Assistance   33

Relocation Assistance   34

Education and Training   37

CONTENTS

Health and Life Insurance 39

Finances 41

Reserve Affiliation 45

Disabled Veterans 45

Individualized Transition Plan (ITP) 46

Retiree Benefits 47

Leaving the Service: Important Points
to Remember 47

At Your Final Out-Processing 49

Chapter 3: VA Benefits and Other Opportunities **51**

Veterans Benefits: A Closer Look 51

Education and Training Benefits 52

Life Insurance Benefits 53

Home Loan Benefits 54

Disability Compensation and Pension
Benefits 55

Vocational Rehabilitation and
Employment Benefits 57

Health Care Benefits 57

Family and Survivor Benefits 58

Burial Benefits 59

Other Benefits 59

Job Training Opportunities 60

Workforce Investment Act 60

Licensing and Certification Information 60

**Entrepreneurship: When You Want to Be
Your Own Boss** 61

Chapter 4: Job Search Necessities   63

Job Search Myths and Realities   64

Establishing a Starting Point   65

Effective Job Search Strategies   66

Think like an employer.   67

Organize your job search campaign.   67

Tap into available job assistance
resources.   70

Identify your work history, marketable
skills, abilities, and experiences.   71

Identify sources of employment
opportunities.   81

Activate your network.   83

Select your references with care.   84

Pitch yourself.   86

Be realistic and reasonable.   86

Chapter 5: Building an Adaptable Resume   89

Why You Need a Resume   89

Five Easy Steps for Designing Your Resume   90

Step One: Identify the focus for your
resume.   91

Step Two: Identify the content and
language for your resume.   96

Step Three: Select the best format to
use.   104

Step Four: Identify additional
experience and include as appropriate.   121

Step Five: Review, edit, and revise your
resume as necessary.   122

What to Do with Your Resume
After You're Hired   123

Resume Writing Tips Worth Reviewing   123

**Chapter 6: Creating Effective Job Search
        Letters   125**

The Parts of a Cover Letter   126

    The Heading   126

    The Dateline   127

    The Addressee   127

    The Salutation   127

    The Introduction   128

    The Main Body   128

    The Conclusion   128

    The Signature Block   130

Thank-You Letters   130

Networking Letters   133

The Letter Resume   135

Get It in Writing   135

The Mechanics of Letter Construction   135

    Letter Size   137

    Typeface Recommendations and
    Enhancements   137

Chapter 7: Winning Interview Skills   139

Understanding the Interview Process   139

    The Informational Interview   139

    The Screening Interview   140

    The Employment Interview   140

    Tips, Techniques, and Tricks of
    the Trade   140

CONTENTS

Before the Interview	**141**
Get your facts straight.	141
Dress for the occasion.	142
Put on a good attitude.	143
Consider the interviewer's perspective.	144
Expand your knowledge of the company.	145
Practice answering common interview questions.	146
Know how to handle potentially illegal questions.	149
Show yourself the money—and the benefits.	150
Prepare your own list of questions.	150
Make up your mind to be yourself.	151
The Day of and During the Interview	**152**
Arrive on time.	152
Be a spy.	152
Be cognizant of your body language.	153
Listen.	154
If you want the job, ask for it.	154
Look into the future.	154
After the Interview	**154**
Send a thank-you note.	155
Follow up.	155
Continue your job search efforts.	156
Chapter 8: Evaluating and Negotiating Job Offers	**157**
Evaluating the Offer	**158**
Do you really want the job?	158

CONTENTS

Can you and the employer come to an
acceptable compensation package? 161

Making the Decision: Using Your Gut 170

Chapter 9: You're Hired! Now What? 173

Wise Words of Advice for Adjusting to
Life on the Job as a Civilian 173

Stop. Look. Listen. Learn. 173

Don't try to change the company
your first week on the job. 174

Don't participate in office gossip—yet. 175

Be considerate of your new colleagues. 175

Don't feel like a task is beneath
your level of expertise. 175

Make yourself indispensable. 176

Keep your eyes open for your next job. 176

Keep your skills current. 177

Be willing to admit to a mistake. 177

Keep your resume updated. 177

In Conclusion... 178

Appendix: Career Transition Resources 181

Index 187

INTRODUCTION

If there's one thing people in the military and those married to it understand, it's the concept of change. We can always count on the fact that things just won't stay the same regardless of our efforts to either resist it or encourage it.

Perhaps the biggest change of all comes when we decide to leave behind the service and its ever-so-eventful lifestyle once and for all. Enter stress, uncertainty, and a general discontent concerning the imminent future that suddenly seems to loom before us in the shape of a huge question mark. To some degree, these feelings are similar to those we have whenever we're handed a new set of orders. A million questions start to form in our minds. Where will I live? Where will I work? How do I find a job?

Those questions only scratch the surface. Clichéd as it may sound, these unsettled feelings are normal to have, regardless of how long you've been in the military or been associated with it as a family member. You may be a "lifer" with an impressive set of rank on your shoulders, and you're getting ready to retire in a year or so. You may think you know it all and have everything under control. After all, you've enjoyed a successful career in the armed forces. You may be a bold, audacious, risk-taking warrior capable of conquering anything, but...do you really know what you have to do in order to actually leave the military?

You thought you had to sign a lot of papers to get in. Just wait and see how much you have to sign to get out! Are you aware of your potential benefits and entitlements as a soon-to-be veteran?

Do you know when you should apply to retire or when you can start a new job? Have you even begun to draft a resume using the English language as opposed to jargon? Or does your resume require the language to which you've become accustomed? Have you begun to transition your professional wardrobe from desert beige to corporate blue?

Maybe you're not the quintessential soldier, sailor, airman, or marine. Maybe you've only been in the military for a short time, and for whatever reason, have been told to leave as soon as possible and don't let the door hit you on the way out. You wouldn't be in a small minority if this is you. Many individuals find that the military is not the right avenue for them. Likewise, the military finds that many individuals aren't right for it, either. This is a recurrent reality, and you just have to decide at some point to get on with your life. Talk about your short-term planning challenges.

Maybe you're content with your career in the armed forces, but an unexpected medical or family hardship situation has surfaced and is the cause for your imminent departure from active duty service. Again, you wouldn't be the first to walk down that road.

Regardless of your situation, you *can* get a grip on what needs to be done and how to do it. That's where the *Military-to-Civilian Career Transition Guide* can help you and your loved ones. This book can help you

- Analyze the choices regarding whether you should stay in the military.

- Prepare for what to expect from those around you as you transition.

- Identify your available military and civilian resources.

- Clarify your potential benefits and entitlements as a soon-to-be veteran.

- Create your overall transition strategy.

- Identify your skills, strengths, weaknesses, and desires.

- Write powerful resumes and cover letters.

- Interview successfully for jobs.

- Effectively evaluate and negotiate job offers.

- Begin your new job with a clear understanding of the civilian side of things.

When it comes to the transition process, it doesn't matter whether you're in the Army, Air Force, Navy, Coast Guard, or Marine Corps. To be sure, each service has its own unique name for different offices or programs. (Ask anyone who has ever been stationed in a joint-service environment how confusing that can be at times.) The basic transition function, however, is the same, and this book can help you wade through the process. Everyone who leaves the military must complete a DD 2648, Preseparation Counseling Checklist, and everyone must be made aware of potential benefits and entitlements. Everyone, at some point, will wake up to see a civilian looking back at him- or herself in the mirror.

The *Military-to-Civilian Career Transition Guide* was written by someone who understands the gritty details of the transition process as well as the range of emotions that are often involved. As a career transition specialist and career center manager for the Army Career and Alumni Program (the Army's transition assistance program, known as ACAP) for nearly eight years, I had the opportunity to assist countless individuals, from *all* branches of the service and in diverse career fields, move from their life with the military into a new civilian existence.

I witnessed many success stories over the years. Success was experienced by those who embraced the transition process and who kept their minds open to new ideas. They were the ones who knew they didn't have all the answers, but they knew which office to visit, which Web site to access, or who to call to get those answers. They were truly empowered and they succeeded. They knew it might not be an easy process, but they held steadfast regardless and found themselves rewarded in the end (or in the beginning, if you will).

The ones who failed did so because they chose to deny the reality of their situations either out of fear, anger, or ignorance. They refused to fully consider their alternatives and they didn't fully utilize the services afforded them. They let obstacles flourish rather than seek solutions to work around them. The old saying that you can lead a horse to water but you can't make him drink is alive and well.

In addition to my professional background, I can also write about this experience from a personal point of view. Throughout the course of preparing this manuscript for you, my active duty Soldier and I experienced our own retirement transition from the military to civilian life, after 21 years and 8 days of PCS'ing all over the world. As I drafted Chapter 1, he drafted his resume. As he interviewed for new jobs, I wrote Chapter 7 about the same subject. As my fearless warrior bravely negotiated the salary for his new job, I crafted Chapter 8 about job evaluation and salary negotiation. We genuinely helped each other out with our individual and joint goals as a result. And yes, he landed a great job with a terrific company, and you can too.

From the personal and the professional perspectives, I can assure you that the transition process can be gut-wrenching, despite how knowledgeable or how prepared you may be for it to happen. There will be high moments and low ones. Just when you feel comfortable with a new set of realities, another offer or circumstance will pop up to make you second-guess yourself. Accept it. It's going to happen, and you may find yourself going over and over the same thoughts until you just want to scream. If you have a spouse and family members, they will want to scream too. Everyone has to remember that this isn't just another move. It's the *big* move and it's important to get it right the first time. (That's why stress management and open communication between family members is especially important during this time of your life!)

It's my sincere hope that you take full advantage of all the resources and services available to you as you chart these new waters, including the use of this book. You and your family are about to embark upon a new chapter in your lives. How exciting is that?

I wish you only the best as you and yours make that transition from the military into civilian life. May your next adventure in life be a grand and successful one!

Janet I. Farley
February 2004

Acknowledgements

The process of writing a book requires motivation, knowledge, dedication, and support. The first three requirements are admirable and well intentioned. Without the support, however, the fruits of one's labor may never find the right audience and that is a tragic thing indeed.

Fortunately, I had support from many individuals, and the idea for this book didn't have to stay swirling around inside my head. I was able to finally get the words down on paper and into your hands, where it is my sincerest hope that you benefit greatly from it. This could not have happened, however, without the interest and commitment from JIST Publishing, Inc. Thanks must go to Mr. Michael Farr for his approval and to Lori Cates Hand, Michael Thomas, Acacia Martinez, and the rest of the staff for their kind assistance along the way.

As I drafted this manuscript, I was also fortunate to hear from a number of individuals (active duty, retired, and separated) who openly shared their feelings, opinions, and experiences with me for the purpose of writing this book. The members of that crowd include Chris Babich, Michael and Patty Holley, Eddie and Judy Wheelock, Eric Binger, Sherry and Steve Martin, Tom Wiederstein and Patty and John Burgin, and Chris and Kevin Hamilton and Susan and Thomas Loden. Thanks to Kathie Hightower, Holly Scherer, T. Walker, Alvin Crawford, Dr. Liz Skinner, and Laurie Davis are also in order.

I am also grateful to Mr. Ramon Vargasortiz of the Mannheim, Germany Transition Center, who kindly reviewed my facts in

Chapter 2 to ensure that they were honest and accurate to the date of his review.

To honestly give credit where credit is due, I must extend my deepest thanks to the Army Career and Alumni Program (ACAP), where I worked for many years as a transition specialist and later as a contract installation manager. During that time, I was afforded the invaluable opportunity to learn everything I ever wanted to know about this topic. More importantly, I was able to pass that knowledge on to others, from all branches of the military wearing varying ranks, who were able to make better decisions in their lives because of it. Nothing is more professionally fulfilling to me than that.

Thanks must also go to Frances and Theresa Farley, whose patience is far greater than their tender ages. A deep debt of gratitude for his support and input is owed to my husband, Therman Farley. As I wrote this book, he and I experienced our own personal military-to-civilian career transition together after 21 years of his service in the U.S. Army. It forced me to really look beyond the professional advice side of my experience and to embrace the genuine feeling side of it as well. I've come full circle on the whole transition issue and I have Farley to thank for that.

Last, but far from least, I thank you. I envy your place in life right now because you are on the verge of a new adventure and nothing can be more exciting than that. It is my deepest hope that you walk away from this book better prepared to handle your own transition. I welcome your comments and/or suggestions at janetfarley@hotmail.com. Godspeed...and get a job.

Dedication

Dedicated with the greatest of love and thanks to
T. A. Farley, Jr., MAJ, U.S. Army, Retired
Frances Taylor Irene Farley
Theresa Anne Farley

CHAPTER 1 Should You Stay or Should You Go?

The sleek multimillion-dollar Madison Avenue advertising campaigns worked just fine on you. Perhaps you were swayed by the "Aim High" Air Force fighter jets bolting across the bright blue morning sky. Or maybe Uncle Sam convinced you that you too might be "one of the few, the proud, the Marines." You might even have been hypnotized by the Navy's state-of-the-art nuclear submarine diving far into the ocean's depths, where no one has ever gone before. Or maybe you decided that you too could be "an Army of one," following in your father's or mother's honorable footsteps. Maybe you were enticed by the promise of paid college tuition and the lure of adventurous travel. Perhaps, like many others, you were influenced by two toppled towers, a smoldering Pentagon, a burned-out field in the middle of nowhere, and a stunned nation one unforgettable September morning in 2001.

For whatever reason, recent or distant past, you joined the United States military. Maybe you put on your uniform over 20 years ago or perhaps you've only worn it for a short while. Regardless of the amount of wear and tear on your BDUs, if you're reading this book, you're probably contemplating the next phase of your life. Before you leap wholeheartedly or reluctantly into that new dimension, make sure you clearly understand what it is you are about to do by fully considering all of your options.

idering All Your Options

e has his or her own story in the military, and you're no exception. Maybe you are an activated reservist who doesn't want to go back to the same old job. Maybe you're at that magical 10-year point where you just know in your gut you have come to a crossroad and must choose one path or the other. Maybe you're a lifer within a few weeks of being able to drop your retirement paperwork, and the lure of the "other side" is starting to do more than just get your attention. Perhaps your contracted tour of duty in the desert, on a rock, or on some remote mountaintop, is nearing an end. You could be on the other end of that scale, without the luxury of choice. Perhaps you were passed over for rank that last time, or a medical condition prevents you from continuing your military service. Perhaps you did something incredibly stupid or sorely misunderstood. Maybe you and Uncle Sam just aren't compatible. All these situations, while different in nature and scope, result in the same outcome: life after the military.

If you have a choice and the luxury of time, don't automatically make a decision one way or the other. Take time to think about the pros and cons involved with a career in the military. Fully explore your options. Seek the advice of subject matter experts around you and make an educated decision that is right for you personally and professionally.

When You Don't Have a Choice in the Matter

Are you absolutely sure that you don't have a choice regarding your stay in the military? Sometimes circumstances can be cloudy, to say the least. If there is any doubt whatsoever in your mind, talk to someone with authority and current knowledge in your food chain at the personnel, legal affairs, chaplain's, or Transition Assistance Office. Don't hesitate to get a second or third opinion on the matter. This is your life and your career. Don't worry about stepping on someone's ego to get the answers you need to make the right decisions for you and your family regarding your future.

After thoroughly investigating your unique situation, if you find that you truly don't have a choice regarding whether you stay in the military, then the decision to leave is an easy one, isn't it? It may not be a pleasant one. It may not be one that you want to have happen in your life or it may be just the ticket you were seeking. In any event, you can truly influence your future success by how you handle this moment in time. As a military outplacement specialist, I've seen people compromise their future possibilities because they were so bitter about being forced to leave the military. They radiated anger and, believe me, potential employers and others that they networked with could sense that negativity. It didn't do them any favors, and it won't help you out, either.

If you are leaving the military under less than pleasant circumstances, choose the high road in your exit. Forget about trying to get back at anyone for ill you may have received. Focus on what you can control and what you can achieve going forward.

What to Know Before You Make It Public Knowledge

If you have come to the definitive decision that you are getting out of the military, then you have reached the internal point of no return. It is now up to you to make your transition as smooth and as profitable for you and your family as possible. You can accomplish this by doing the following:

- **Get a grip on your new reality.** Accept the fact that you and your family will be stressed about this transition regardless of how well you execute the whole process. Change is stressful. Develop a plan for keeping blood pressure levels low. It doesn't have to be an elaborate plan. It just has to work. Walk the dog, work out, go for a jog, engage yourself in a self-absorbing hobby or anything that will help you keep things in perspective.

- **Create an overall transition plan that works for you.** Your Transition Assistance Office will provide you with a standard framework for this, but it's up to you to customize it. Moreover, it's up to you to actually work that plan. No one is going to hold your hand throughout this process, so don't expect that for one minute.

- **Study up on your job-hunting skills.** Even if you have previous experience in the job search process, take advantage of the free services offered you by the military as you leave it. Taking advantage of these services will allow you to network with others who are going through the same experience. Additionally, it will connect you to professionals who are likewise connected to employers seeking qualified candidates for positions. It's a win-win opportunity. Don't let it slip by just because you think you know everything about job hunting already.

- **Learn the skills necessary to help you manage your new career.** Your next job won't be the result of "another PCS move." It will be your new job, maybe your first job, in a totally new work culture. Step gently until you have a real feel for the environment.

The Hardest Thing About Leaving the Military

Paperwork? Sure, there's no shortage of it when you decide to get out. Everything you sign will have some major importance to it and need to be filed away for some future reason. Organizational skills are a definite must for the transitioner! Paperwork is not, however, the hardest thing about leaving the military. Sentimentality? You wouldn't be the first person to get a funny feeling in the pit of your stomach when it finally hits you that you're leaving behind the comfort of a strangely self-contained world. Writing what may be your first resume ever? (No, you don't have to label it "Unclassified" at the top of the page.) Updating your wardrobe? (Shockingly, green, black, brown, and blue are not the only shades on the color wheel.)

Finding your next source of income? That's a hard one, but not the hardest.

All of these things represent real challenges when you decide to leave behind your camouflaged lifestyle, but the hardest thing about leaving the military might surprise you. You will, however, recognize it in an instant when you experience it. It involves the people you work with or report to every day. What you will most likely discover is that your chain of command and your peers or co-workers don't want you to leave.

Family Voices

We are planning on making our transition shortly after he returns from his one-year deployment to Iraq. Our concerns at this point in our lives are the unknowns of what is ahead. At this point, we are saving all we can for retirement. We own our own home and have less than 10 years to pay it off. Our only child just turned nine years old, so stability and roots are becoming important to us right now also.
—Patty Burgin, Military Spouse Extraordinaire

Now, that may sound touching, but it's not. They know that the workload goes on even when you leave, and they will be left to bear it. Warm bodies, as you know, are a real commodity in the military. There just aren't as many of them as there used to be. Those living, breathing human resources will be forced to take up the workload from those who move on (that would be you), at least until new blood is assigned to the unit or until your replacement hits the same competency level that you are taking with you. Maybe you have even experienced this yourself when others have left the military. Those who you work with will either provide you with the emotional and real-world support you need to get your transition together, or they will rather unpoetically dump every last dirty job on you to complete before your exit.

It's not always just those you work with, either. Your best friend, your spouse, or even your kids can quickly let you know in subtle ways (or not) that your change in direction is not necessarily a welcome one for their personal security levels.

So where does this get you? One step ahead of the process if you realize that others may not share in your enthusiasm for a future *sans* uniform. You can try to reason with the offended parties and hope that they understand your situation. Don't count on it working out smoothly with everyone. Just know that you will have to find some way to deal with this resistance when it hits you square in the face.

Anticipating the Culture Shock

You are leaving a completely self-contained environment for one that is not quite so clear cut. Will it be different? Oh, yes. Even if you work for the government after you get out, things will be different.

When you wear your uniform, you possess an automatic status within the culture. In a sense, you wear your resume. Someone can look at the patch on your sleeve and see which unit you belong to. The rank you wear on your shoulder or on your lapel tells someone (theoretically, at least) what level of responsibility you carry. Everyone in uniform generally has a well-kept haircut and enjoys a certain level of physical fitness.

As a civilian, you can let your hair grow, get an earring in your nose, and gain those extra 10 pounds if you want to. No first sergeant or commander is going to tell you to remove them. No civilian is going to salute you as you walk down the street. And forget about showing your ID card at the local grocery store. You'll discover that, unlike in post or base housing, you can keep your yard any way your heart desires. Your neighbors probably won't care unless you bring down the property values around you. Things will also be different on the job.

When you leave the service, don't be surprised if you find yourself feeling a little at odds over your new lifestyle. Chances are that you may even find yourself in mourning over your new civilian status, even if you wanted to get out of uniform more than anything in the world. That may sound odd, but it's not uncommon. You may experience some or all of the typically recognized stages of grief such as denial and isolation, anger, bargaining, depression, acceptance, and finally, hope. To effectively manage these stages, it's critical that you establish attainable goals, communicate clearly and often with those around you, and diligently work your transition plan.

Perhaps the best strategy for dealing with any of these stages is to confront head-on any obstacles that come your way. Don't ignore potential problems that could fester and morph into nasty monsters. Remember that you have a support network available. You might find comfort and solace from any number of sources when tough times hit by turning to your spouse, your children, your golfing buddies, your chaplain, or a trusted friend. The Family Service Centers and the Transition Assistance Offices near you also offer concrete advice for turning dismal situations around with the assistance of positive action.

Focus on the Family

As the person in uniform, it's easy to focus on yourself during the transition. If you are blessed with a spouse and/or a family, it's crucial that you include them in the whole process from start to finish.

Perhaps your family has been by your side for years and has endured countless transfers and untold heartache along with the good. It's not easy being married to the military, as anyone in that position can tell you. Be sure you keep those lines of communication open between you and the family during this critical juncture in your lives. It may not be easy on everyone, and you need to be able to see that storm coming before it happens. Honestly and openly share your feelings with one another and fully consider the needs and wants of each member of your family. You're in this together, just as you have always been.

CHAPTER 2 | Creating Your Overall Transition Strategy

Transition. Think about it. When was the last time you weren't already living some type of transition as a member of the armed forces family? In all reality, you probably can't remember when you weren't experiencing change. That's the very nature of the military beast. The saving grace here is that you can use the skills you've always called upon to adapt and to succeed with this particular transition despite it having a vastly different destination.

In your military career, you never embarked on any mission without prior planning. This mission is certainly no different. You're at a critical point where you need to do two things. First, you need to know your end game. In other words, where do you see yourself after this transition? This involves more than just knowing where; it involves developing a detailed timeline outlining your plan to get there. Second, you need to work that timeline by gathering as much information as possible so you can make educated decisions along the way. Picture this framework in your mind and set it up on a piece of paper, in your handheld, or on your computer. Refer to it daily. Make sure your progress is just that, and not idle waiting and wishing.

Your End Game and Transition Timeline

Where do you see yourself when you get out of the military? In a similar job with a civilian employer? In a totally different career field? Being your own boss? Asking the customer if they'd like fries with that order? If you haven't already done so, you certainly need to give this topic some thought. You need to have an idea of where you want to be in the end. That's not to say that you will achieve that end result with the first job interview or even within the first year. It is a goal that you will plan for and work towards.

In addition to having that goal, you must mix in a healthy dose of reality. For example, what are your immediate employment needs? Do you have a family that has to be taken care of and a mortgage that has to be paid on time? Do you have a sufficient financial cushion to allow you the luxury of time in your job search, or do you need to get hired as soon as possible to keep the money flowing comfortably?

There aren't any right or wrong answers here. Everyone will have their own take on the subject. Only you can determine what you need to initially focus on for your unique situation. The *ideal* situation is that you can take your time looking for that perfect job and not accept anything less. The *reality* is that you sometimes need to take a decent job, get used to being a civilian again, and discreetly continue your job search. This doesn't mean that you abandon your goal. In fact, it means that you work even harder to see it materialize.

The Ever-Burning Question Remains: What Do You Do When in the Transition Process?

It would be easy if you were issued a crystal ball and could simply predict the future; however, there's no fun in that, is there? Because everyone has his or her own situation, timelines for transition will likewise differ.

- If you plan to retire from the military, you should start preparing at the two- or three-years-out mark. At that point, retirement may still seem a long way off, but it's not. It will hit you in the face before you know it. The longer you have to contemplate and set up your post-uniform move, the better for you and your family.

- If you are retiring or voluntarily separating from service, your actual transition should begin at the one-year-out mark. Again, you may find that this notion is not always wholly supported within the military food chain, but it's still the ideal. If you're contemplating retirement, it's a necessity. If you're voluntarily separating, the next best plan is the six-months-out time frame; however, a year is still ideal.

- If you are being involuntarily separated from the military, your timeline gets a bit complicated. You might find yourself out of the service within one year, one month, one week, or 48 hours, depending upon your circumstances. You don't always know how much time you're going to have to process your transition and begin your job search. Your future is in someone else's hands, and it's disturbing to say the least.

If you find yourself in this situation, then you must exercise extra diligence in planning your transition and implementing it. Suppose, for example, you are going to be separated from the military because of a medical condition. You have a period of time when you are waiting to see what the medical board is going to determine about your case. The end result could be that you have to exit the military within 90 days from the date of the approved medical message. On the other hand, the end result could demand that you remain on active duty despite your situation. You don't know and you won't know until the findings are presented to you. In this case, if you wait for the results from the medical board to plan your transition, write your resume, and research the job market, you will find that you are way behind the power curve if you are forced to leave the service. For your own benefit, you have to move forward with the process as if you were leaving the service. If it turns out that you don't go, then you've lost nothing. You've completed a dry run for that time when you do transition.

This is critical. Don't let your emotions hinder your clear judgment. You wouldn't do so while on duty; don't do so while planning your future.

Having said that, it's time now to look at exactly what needs to be taken care of during your transition and when you should take care of it. We're going to assume, for the purpose of this proposed timeline, that you have at least six months to aggressively implement the tasks in this plan. If you have more or less time available, then you must adjust the timeline to fit your schedule.

Preseparation Timeline Activities Checklist

Days Before Separation	Activity	Resources to Assist You	Scheduled	Completed
730–365	If applicable, make the decision whether to retire or not. If you do, make sure your voluntary retirement is accepted by your branch of service within service guidelines. Include your family in the decision.	Personnel Office, Transition Assistance Office	☐	☐
365–300	If retiring, provide the Transition Assistance Office with an approved copy of your retirement.	Transition Assistance Office	☐	☐

(continued)

(continued)

Days Before Separation	Activity	Resources to Assist You	Scheduled	Completed
180	Schedule and attend mandatory Preseparation Counseling with your spouse, if you have one.	Transition Assistance Office	☐	☐
180	Complete your DD 2648, Preseparation Counseling Checklist, with the assistance of a career counselor.	Transition Assistance Office	☐	☐
180	Attend a Transition Assistance Workshop. Your spouse can also benefit from this workshop.	Transition Assistance Office	☐	☐
180	Develop your unique job search strategy and begin researching the job market.	Transition Assistance Office	☐	☐

Days Before Separation	Activity	Resources to Assist You	Scheduled	Completed
180	Objectively assess your skills and interests by taking a vocational interest inventory.	Education Center	☐	☐
180	Review and make a copy of your personnel records.	Personnel Office	☐	☐
180	Have a family meeting and jointly discuss potential job and living locations.	You and your immediate family	☐	☐
180	If you are stationed overseas and wish to remain there after separation, obtain approval to do so.	Personnel Office	☐	☐

(continued)

(continued)

Days Before Separation	Activity	Resources to Assist You	Scheduled	Completed
180	Begin assembling a civilian wardrobe suitable for employment purposes.	Transition Assistance Office, personal shoppers at reputable stores	☐	☐
180	Determine your permissive TDY and transition leave options.	Personnel Office	☐	☐
150	Begin networking with everyone.	Friends, family, colleagues, and new contacts	☐	☐
150	Attend job fairs to meet contacts and gather job leads and employer information.	Transition Assistance Office	☐	☐

Days Before Separation	Activity	Resources to Assist You	Scheduled	Completed
150	Develop alternate plans of action as a backup.	You and your immediate family	☐	☐
150	Continue researching the job market, targeting specific locations and opportunities.	Job search and relocation Web sites,[1] networking contacts, newspapers	☐	☐
150	Stress check: Are you doing okay? If not, seek the assistance of available resources.	Family Center, Chaplain's Office, family and/or friends	☐	☐
150	Establish and/or review your financial plan to see you through this transition.	You, your immediate family, and/ or your financial planner or advisor	☐	☐

[1] See the Appendix for an extensive listing of helpful Web sites.

(continued)

(continued)

Days Before Separation	Activity	Resources to Assist You	Scheduled	Completed
150	If you are under obligation to do so, join the Reserves.[2]	Reserve Component Career Counselor	☐	☐
120	Request Your Verification of Military Experience and Training (DD Form 2586) to assist you in preparing your resume.	Order online at www.dmdc.osd.mil/vmet	☐	☐
120	Draft your resume and have a career counselor review it and offer suggestions/comments.	Transition Assistance Office and/or Family Service Center	☐	☐
120	Pull together your federal employment packet if you are considering this avenue of employment.	Civilian Personnel Office, Transition Assistance Office	☐	☐

[2] If you have not completed eight years of active-duty service in the military, you should schedule an appointment with the Reserve Component Career Counselor to clarify your remaining obligation to the military and potential options available to you.

Days Before Separation	Activity	Resources to Assist You	Scheduled	Completed
120	Explore your relocation options and entitlements.	Relocation Assistance Office and online at www.dmdc.osd.mil/sites	☐	☐
120	Continue with your networking campaign.	Friends, family, colleagues, and new contacts	☐	☐
120	If living in government quarters, inquire about clearing procedures.[3]	Housing Office	☐	☐
120	Clarify your educational benefits and entitlements.[4]	Education Office	☐	☐

[3]In rare circumstances only, separating service members may have the option to stay in housing for a limited time at their own expense. Talk to your housing office for more information.

[4]See Chapter 3, "VA Benefits and Other Opportunities," for more information about your potential educational benefits and entitlements.

(continued)

(continued)

Days Before Separation	Activity	Resources to Assist You	Scheduled	Completed
120	If you plan to attend college after your separation, find out what admittance exams may be required by the school you wish to attend.[5]	Education Office, Student Affairs Office at the school of your choice	☐	☐
120	Clarify your transitional health care entitlements.[6]	Transition Assistance Office	☐	☐

[5] Don't forget that some required exams (i.e., GMAT, GRE) as well as optional exams such as CLEP are usually available at the Education Center and do not cost you anything as an active-duty service member. Test before you take off your uniform!

[6] The Transition Office actually clarifies your eligibility for this benefit. The Health Care Advisor at the military medical treatment facility can give you details about the actual programs.

Days Before Separation	Activity	Resources to Assist You	Scheduled	Completed
120	Schedule a separation physical even if it is not a requirement for your transition.[7]	Medical Treatment Facility	☐	☐
90	Begin applying for jobs using the final version of your resume targeted to specific opportunities and conduct follow-up calls/visits.[8]	Career and employer Web sites, newspapers, firms	☐	☐
90	Pull together your interview outfit.	Transition Assistance Office, your own sound judgment (or your spouse's!)	☐	☐

[7] If you are retiring or separating because of a medical condition, a physical exam is required. It is free health care. Take advantage of it!

[8] See chapters 4 through 8 for specific job search strategies and guidance.

(continued)

(continued)

Days Before Separation	Activity	Resources to Assist You	Scheduled	Completed
90	Request your Verification of Military Experience.	Order online at www.dmdc. osd.mil/vmet.	☐	☐
90	Continue with your networking campaign.	Friends, family, colleagues, and new contacts	☐	☐
90	If retiring, schedule and attend an SBP briefing. Your spouse, if you have one, is required to attend.	Retirement Services Office or Transition Assistance Office if you are stationed overseas	☐	☐
90	Schedule an appointment to clarify your shipment and storage of household goods potential benefits and entitlements.	Transportation Office	☐	☐

Days Before Separation	Activity	Resources to Assist You	Scheduled	Completed
90	Schedule a final dental exam.[9]	Dental Facility	☐	☐
90	Find out if you are eligible for separation pay.	Transition Assistance Office	☐	☐
90	Prepare or update your will if necessary.[10]	Legal Office	☐	☐
60	Aggressively continue your networking and job search activities.	Friends, family, colleagues, and new contacts	☐	☐

[9] If time doesn't permit you to do this, make sure that the dental facility notes so on your final clearance. The VA will allow for a one-time cleaning and exam up to 90 days after your separation, if you did not do so within the 90 days before your separation.

[10] This service is free while you are in on active-duty status. If you are retiring, you should still be eligible to use the services of the Legal Office free of charge even after you separate. If you are not retiring, you would need to pay for such services. Again, use them before you lose them!

(continued)

23

(continued)

Days Before Separation	Activity	Resources to Assist You	Scheduled	Completed
60	Inquire about your potential Veterans Benefits.	Transition Assistance Office, VA Representatives, or online at www.va.gov	☐	☐
30	Visit the area where you plan to live after separation.	Chamber of Commerce, Relocation Assistance Office, online at www.dmdc.osd.mil/sites	☐	☐
30	Continue to aggressively network and apply for jobs.	Friends, family, colleagues, and new contacts	☐	☐

Days Before Separation	Activity	Resources to Assist You	Scheduled	Completed
30	Review your all-important Certificate of Release or Discharge from Active Duty (DD Form 214) for accuracy as well as any other required documents.	Transition Assistance Office	☐	☐
30	If unemployed, inquire about unemployment compensation benefits.	Department of Labor	☐	☐
30	Copy and review your medical and dental records.	Medical/ Dental Facilities	☐	☐
30	If retiring, plan your retirement ceremony.	Plan to your own taste and budget	☐	☐

(continued)

(continued)

Days Before Separation	Activity	Resources to Assist You	Scheduled	Completed
30	Complete your Veterans Affairs Disability Application (VA Form 21-526).	Obtain form online at www.va.gov or visit the Transition Assistance Office or a VA office.	☐	☐
30	Investigate the pros and cons of converting your SGLI to VGLI.	VA representative, Transition Assistance Office	☐	☐
7	If retiring, begin the process of obtaining your new ID cards.	Personnel Office, Retirement Services		

Once you have a guideline to follow, it's critical that you do so. Only by literally checking off the boxes will you ensure that you have covered the important areas concerning your transition. All of the items on the Preseparation Timeline Activities Checklist may not apply to you. There may be others that you should add according to your own unique situation. Photocopy and use the guideline as is or creatively revise it so it's tailored to you. It's your guideline and you should do whatever it takes to make it work for you.

Military Transition Assistance

As you read over the timeline, note one recurring theme: Transition Assistance Office.

I can't stress enough how important it is that you visit this office as soon as possible. Even if you have only the vaguest notion of leaving the military, visit the professionals who work here and start getting answers to your questions. Visiting the office alone does not commit you to getting out of the military. If you're concerned that your presence there might send the wrong message to your colleagues or to your boss, call or e-mail the office instead of visiting it. Most counselors will be happy to answer your questions or point you in the right direction over the phone or by e-mail. You might also try visiting during your lunch hour versus taking time off from work.

The point is this: You can only make an educated decision about your future if you get the answers to your questions first. You might discover, after thoroughly investigating the job market, that staying in the military is a better option for you at this time. You would never be able to come to that conclusion had you not researched the issue. Or, quite the opposite, your findings might reinforce your belief that it's time to switch employers.

Visiting the Transition Assistance Office

You may know where to find your local Transition Assistance Office already. If not, the following information may help:

- If you're in the **Army,** visit the Army Career and Alumni Program (ACAP). (They will facilitate your preseparation counseling and refer you to the Transition Assistance Office.)

- If you're in the **Air Force,** visit the Transition Assistance Staff or Career Consultant at the Family Support Center.

- If you're in the **Navy,** visit your Command Career Counselor at the Fleet and Family Support Center.

- If you're in the **Marine Corps,** visit your Career Resource Management Center Specialist at the Personal Services Center (formerly the Family Services Center).

- If you're in the **Coast Guard,** visit the Work-Life Staff.

For this book, the generic term "Transition Assistance Office" will be used to indicate the above locations. To locate any Transition Assistance Office worldwide, hop on the Internet and access the Department of Defense Transportal Web page at www.dodtransportal.org. This is an excellent starting point to gain an overview of the entire transition process. Using the Web page, you can locate any Transition Assistance Office in the world, based on your branch of service. It also provides you with an online version of the Preseparation Guide, a DOD handbook providing information on various services and benefits available to separating service members and their families. (The Preseparation Guide is also known as DA Pam 635-4, NAVMC 2916, AFJMAN 36-2128, or NAVPERS 15616.) The most recent edition of the guide (as of the printing of this book) is October 2001. It is a *must-read* for every transitioner.

After you contact your Transition Assistance Office, then what? The professionals who work there know that knowledge is critical to your future success, and that's what they can provide you. They are the ones who will usually facilitate your mandatory preseparation counseling, which involves completing your DD 2648, Preseparation Counseling Checklist.

Your Preseparation Counseling Checklist

At first glance, you might believe DD 2648 to be just another form that you have to fill out and sign in order to further your trek to separation. It is not. It is a required form that becomes a part of your permanent personnel file. By signing it, you tell Uncle Sam that you are aware that certain potential benefits and entitlements may be due you.

Quite likely, if you do not have your DD 2648 at your final clearing point, you will not be cleared. You will be sent to the Transition Assistance Office for proof that you have received your mandatory preseparation counseling, and that proof comes in the form of DD 2648.

The form itself (see pages 30–31) resembles a checklist loaded with various talking points that are vital to your future. You will be required to check YES or NO after each point to indicate your interest in obtaining more information on a given topic. It won't hurt you to check YES on everything, even if something doesn't apply to you. Checking NO will not prevent you from receiving an entitlement if you are honestly due it.

After you have been briefed, either by a counselor or by a computer talking head, you will be given a list of service providers and asked to sign the form. You will be permitted a copy; the transition office may keep a copy or two. Each transition office may have its own procedures; just remember that you need to get this block checked off in your exit process without fail.

It's also important to remember that the burden of getting the answers to your many questions lies only with you. You are given the tools (the basic information and the service provider contact numbers), and it is up to you, not the folks at Transition, to get the answers to the questions you have. If you happen to get answers that are confusing, ask someone else for clarification. It's worth the extra effort, and it could mean the difference between receiving a benefit due you or not.

PRESEPARATION COUNSELING CHECKLIST

(Please read Privacy Act Statement below before completing this form.)

SECTION I - PRIVACY ACT STATEMENT

AUTHORITY: 10 USC 1142, E.O. 9397.

PRINCIPAL PURPOSE(S): To record preseparation services and benefits requested by and provided to Service members; to identify preseparation counseling areas of interest as a basis for development of an Individual Transition Plan (ITP). The signed preseparation counseling checklist will be maintained in the Service member's official personnel file. Title 10, USC 1142, requires that not later than 90 days before the date of separation, preseparation counseling for Service members be made available.

ROUTINE USE(S): None.

DISCLOSURE: Voluntary; however, it will not be possible to initiate preseparation services or develop an Individual Transition Plan (ITP) for a Service member if the information is not provided.

SECTION II - PERSONAL INFORMATION *(To be filled out by all applicants)*

1. NAME *(Last, First, Middle Initial)*		2. SSN	3. GRADE
4. SERVICE	**5. DUTY STATION**	**6. EXPECTED SEPARATION DATE** *(YYYYMMDD)*	**7. DATE CHECKLIST PREPARED** *(YYYYMMDD)*

SECTION III. ALL TRANSITIONING SERVICE MEMBERS MUST READ AND SIGN.

I was offered preseparation counseling on the above date (Item 7) on my transition benefits and services as appropriate. I understand that this preseparation counseling is provided to assist my transition process as required by Title 10, USC 1142.

I ☐ accept ☐ decline *(X appropriate block)* further transition assistance counseling. *(If you declined further transition assistance counseling, sign and date.)* I have checked those items where I desire further information or counseling. I have also been advised where to obtain assistance in developing an Individual Transition Plan (ITP).

8a. SERVICE MEMBER SIGNATURE	b. DATE *(YYYYMMDD)*	9a. TRANSITION COUNSELOR SIGNATURE	b. DATE *(YYYYMMDD)*

SECTION IV. Please indicate *(by checking YES or NO)* whether you *(or your spouse if applicable)* desire counseling for the following services and benefits. All benefits and services checked YES should be used in developing your ITP. The following services and benefits are available to all Service members, unless otherwise specified:

	SERVICE MEMBER			SPOUSE			REFERRED TO *(Input is optional)*
	YES	NO	N/A	YES	NO	N/A	
10. EFFECTS OF A CAREER CHANGE							
11. EMPLOYMENT ASSISTANCE							
a. Dept. of Labor sponsored Transition Assistance Workshops and Service sponsored Transition Seminars/Workshops							
b. Use of DD Form 2586 (Verification of Military Experience and Training)							
(1) Do you want a copy of your Verification of Military Experience and Training (VMET) Document? If yes, go to http://www.dmdc.osd.mil/vmet to download your VMET document.							
c. DoD Job Search Web site: dod.jobsearch.org							
d. Transition Bulletin Board (TBB) and Public and Community Service Opportunities (http://www.dmdc.osd.mil/ot/)							
e. Teacher and Teacher's Aide Opportunities/Troops to Teachers (http://voled.doded.mil/dantes/ttt)							
f. Federal Employment Opportunities							
g. Hiring Preference in Non-Appropriated Fund (NAF) jobs (Eligible Involuntary Separatees)							
h. State Employment Agencies/America's Job Bank							
12. RELOCATION ASSISTANCE *NOTE: Status of Forces Agreement limitations apply for overseas Service members.*							
a. Permissive (TDY/TAD) and Excess leave							
*b. Travel and transportation allowances							
13. EDUCATION/TRAINING							
a. Education benefits (Montgomery GI Bill, Veterans Educational Assistance Program, Vietnam-era, etc.)							
b. Workforce Investment Act (WIA)							
c. Additional education or training options							

DD FORM 2648, JUL 2002   PREVIOUS EDITION MAY BE USED.

Preseparation Counseling Checklist.

PRESEPARATION COUNSELING CHECKLIST **SECTION IV** *(Continued)*	NAME *(Last, First, Middle Initial)*						SSN

	SERVICE MEMBER			SPOUSE			REFERRED TO
	YES	NO	N/A	YES	NO	N/A	*(Input is optional)*
13. EDUCATION/TRAINING *(Continued)*							
d. Licensing and Certification Information (www.umet-vets.dol.gov)							
e. Defense Activity for Non-Traditional Educational Support (www.voled.doded.mil/)							
14. HEALTH AND LIFE INSURANCE							
a. 60-day or 120-day extended Military and limited Dental benefits (Eligible Involuntary Separatees)							
b. Option to purchase 18-month conversion health insurance. Concurrent pre-existing condition coverage with purchase of conversion health insurance.							
c. Veterans' Group Life Insurance							
15. FINANCES							
a. Financial Management (TSP, Retirement, SBP)							
b. Separation pay (Eligible Involuntary Separatees)							
c. Unemployment compensation							
d. Other financial assistance (VA Loans, SBA Loans, and other government grants and loans)							
16. RESERVE AFFILIATION							
17. DISABLED VETERANS BENEFITS							
a. Disabled Transition Assistance Program (DTAP)							
b. VA Disability Benefits							
18. INDIVIDUAL TRANSITION PLAN (ITP)							

a. As a separating Service member, after receiving basic preparation counseling information and completing this checklist, you and your spouse (if applicable) are entitled to receive assistance in developing an Individual Transition Plan (ITP) based on the areas of interest you have identified on this checklist. The preseparation counseling checklist addresses a variety of transition services and benefits to which you may be entitled. Each individual is strongly encouraged to take advantage of the opportunity to develop an ITP. The purpose of the ITP is to identify educational, training and employment objectives and to develop a plan to help you achieve these objectives. It is the Military Department's responsibility to offer Service members the opportunity and assistance to develop an ITP. It is the Service member's responsibility to develop an ITP based on his/her specific objectives and the objectives of his or her spouse, if appropriate.

b. Based upon information received during Preseparation Counseling, do you desire assistance in developing your ITP? If yes, the Transition staff/Command Career Counselor is available to assist you.							

SECTION V - REMARKS

DD FORM 2648 (BACK), JUL 2002

31

Stress

As we've already discussed, life is different outside the military. With any change, be it a duty station or a transition out, there will be stress.

Stress is something you and your family can probably write your own book on at this point. While there is no getting around stress, you can, as you may already know, get around the effects of it. There will be many unknowns in your transition, and you have a choice regarding how you handle those unknowns. You can let stress get to you or you can do something to ease the pain of it.

Dare I say it, you can implement your own stress management plan. One component of this plan might include using the services of your local family center, family support groups, the chaplain's office, or the installation's mental health facility. There are a number of excellent self-help books on the market (and at your installation's library) that can give you pointers for dealing with tumultuous times. You can also combat stress with activities such as

- Working out

- Going for a walk

- Delving into a creative process to occupy your mind and senses

- Talking things over with your spouse and family members

You can beat stress by separating yourself from it for a little while and clearing your head. At that point, you can look more objectively and not emotionally at the issue and develop options for solving it if possible.

Been There, Done That, Got the T-Shirt

I think that the husband and the wife should work through the [transition] process together. It's easy for me, the military member, to go over to the Transition Assistance Office and to go to all the related briefings. I'm sorry to say that I didn't do it right. It should be a joint endeavor; it involves the two of you. It may be hard when you both are working, but this is a stressful time in both of your lives. The more you do as a couple can surely help the transition process.

—Michael Holley, LTC, USA (Ret.)

Being stressed isn't necessarily a bad thing. It allows you to recognize that there are issues in your life causing you angst. By recognizing that they exist, you can take care of them appropriately. After all, "stressed" spelled backwards is "desserts." That can't be all bad, can it?

Employment Assistance

Are you going to want a job after you leave the military? The answer may be "Yes, of course. There are bills to pay and mouths to feed." Or it may be, "Not right away." Perhaps you will be attending college on a full-time basis, or maybe you just want to take a few months off to relax.

Regardless of which category you fall under, you should check a resounding YES at the employment assistance. Knowing how to research the job market and find a job is a skill you cannot do without. Maybe you already have a good idea how to get a job. Great. Take advantage of the services that are offered to you by the military anyway. Trained outplacement professionals, in unison with Department of Labor experts, might still be able to teach you a thing or two, and that will make it all worthwhile.

In addition to learning how to conduct a successful job search and all that it implies (resumes, cover letters, interviewing skills, applications, etc.), the Transition Assistance Office is an excellent networking station for you. (See "Visiting the Transition Assistance Office" above for more details regarding potential services.)

As you transition out, you should also request a Verification of Military Training and Experience (also known as VMET or DD Form 2586). This is an official document that verifies the military training you have had and assigns it recommended college-level credit. It is not to be confused with your military transcript discussed in the "Education and Training" section below. You will want a copy of your VMET primarily to assist you in preparing your resume. You can obtain a copy of your transcript at www.dmdc.osd.mil/vmet.

As you will learn in the transition office–sponsored workshops, there are a number of places out there to seek a job. For example, the DOD Job Search Web site (http://dod.jobsearch.org) is an excellent place to begin your job-hunting activities. The Defense Manpower's Data Center also posts private industry as well as public and community service opportunities on the Transition Bulletin Board (TBB) at www.dmdc.osd.mil/ot. Those interested in teaching opportunities (i.e., Troops to Teachers) should visit http://voled.doded.mil/ dantes/ttt. Federal opportunities may be found at www.usajobs. opm.gov. A listing of the individual federal agencies having service opportunities is provided in this book's appendix. Non-appropriated fund jobs are also available on individual military installations and should be explored as well. Finally, state employment agencies post their jobs on America's Job Bank at www.americasjobbank.com.

Relocation Assistance

Your transition out of the military may or may not involve a move. If it does, then you certainly want to get all the scoops on the subject. Even if you're already settled somewhere and don't foresee a move, you never know.

If you want to get an idea about future potential locations to live, an excellent resource to reference is the Standardized Installation Topic Exchange System (SITES) database. You can access it online at www.dmdc.osd.mil/SITES. This is an extensive listing of every American military installation in the world.

What's that? Why would you choose to look at military bases again? If you are retiring, you might want to live within reasonable commuting distance of a military installation to take advantage of your retiree benefits. Even if you're not retiring, military installations represent viable sources of employment. The SITES database gives you a broad overview of a number of topics:

- The installation itself
- Educational opportunities
- Employment possibilities
- Relocation services
- Child care and teen activities
- Facts at a glance list
- The local community (off base or post)
- Medical and dental services
- Housing
- Support services
- Survival tips

SITES is definitely worth a look.

With any relocation, remember that *cost of living* is a big deal. You might be thrilled to accept a job in Washington, DC, but if the salary offered doesn't take into consideration the astronomical cost of living in that area, you might find yourself struggling to make ends meet. To learn more about cost-of-living fluctuations, consult such online calculators as

- www.homefair.com
- money.cnn.com
- www.salary.com

Once you receive your orders to separate, you need to visit the transportation office to inquire about household shipment and/or storage procedures. As you well know, during peak travel months it can be difficult to get convenient moving dates set up for you and your family. The military will move you and your family back to your listed home of record free of charge. If you want to move somewhere else, they will cover the cost up to the amount it would have cost to move you to your home of record. You (or perhaps your new employer?) pick up the rest of the tab.

If you are retiring, you are authorized to move once anywhere in the continental United States, compliments of Uncle Sam. If you live overseas and wish to remain there, you may request an extension of this benefit for a period of time. Consult your transition and/or transportation office for more information on relocation and storage of goods.

Maybe you are one of the brave souls who choose to do a Do-It-Yourself move (DITY). Good for you. Before you break your grandmother's irreplaceable china, find out how much the military will reimburse you for such damages. (At this printing, the rate was 95 percent.)

Another relevant topic within the relocation discussion involves such potential benefits as permissive travel (TDY/TAD) to house hunt or job hunt. You may or may not be permitted this benefit. If you are being involuntarily separated, you could be afforded up to 20 days if you are stationed in the continental United States (CONUS) or 30 days if you are stationed outside the continental United States (OCONUS) and relocating back to CONUS or to another OCONUS location. If you are retiring, you could be authorized travel anywhere in the United States. If you are leaving the military because you have fulfilled the requirements of your contract, you will not be eligible for this benefit.

You will also want to take a look at any excess leave you may have accumulated. You may have the option of selling it back to the government. Bear in mind, however, you will be taxed on the money you receive. If you are retiring or going into the reserves, you should have future commissary and post or base exchange benefits. (Note to future retirees wishing to live overseas and use such services: Depending upon your employment status, you may be required to pay additional country tax on items purchased at the commissary and exchanges through the installation's customs office.)

Let's not forget the kids. If you have a child who is a senior at a Department of Defense Dependent School (DODDS) you may be eligible to have your child graduate from that school. You may have to pay tuition for it to actually happen. Contact the DODDS directly for more information.

Education and Training

Before you take off your uniform, you want to know exactly what educational and training benefits are available or due to you.

One stop you need to make is at your local Education Center. If you have paid into the Montgomery GI Bill, you will want to know how to take advantage of that program. If you participated in a past program (i.e., Veterans Educational Assistance Program [VEAP]) and wish to convert your benefit to the Montgomery GI Bill, you still may be able to do so. Benefits and methods for getting them periodically change, but one constant is this: You have only 10 years after you separate to use them. Don't lose them.

The experts at the Education Center should be able to give you the most recent news concerning your benefits. An equally excellent place to look is online at the Veterans Affairs Benefits page. The Web address is www.va.gov. Chapter 3, "VA Benefits and Other Opportunities," can also give you more details on this topic.

The Department of Labor is also one place you will want to visit as you transition, for a couple of reasons. One, they are the place to find out about local and state employment opportunities. They are highly connected to the community. For you, that means that they can help you network your way into a job. Two, they can point you in the direction of additional training opportunities such as the Workforce Investment Act (WIA).

You can learn about various licensing and certification requirements by accessing www.umet-vets.dol.gov.

Other services provided by your Education Center include testing (CLEP, ACT, SAT, GRE, GMAT, and other standardized tests) free of charge while you are on active duty. Keep in mind that test results are generally good for a decent period of time. (For example, test scores for the GRE are available up to five years after you take the test.) So, even if you are not planning to go back to school for that master's degree just now, take the GRE or GMAT because it doesn't cost you anything while you wear the uniform. As a civilian, one test could easily cost you $100. There is always the dreaded possibility that you would need to take the test more than once. To explore this topic in more detail, log on to the Defense Activity for Non-Traditional Education Support Web site at www.voled.doded.mil.

If you don't know what you want to be when you grow up, the Education Center can offer you a number of vocational and interest assessments and inventories. It never hurts to consider alternatives.

Finally, before you transition from the military, request a copy of your transcript (see the following table). Yes, you have one. All those military schools and/or courses you attended will show up on it as well as the American Council on Education's recommendation of how many college credits it could be worth. This might come in handy if you pursue an associate's, a bachelor's, or even a master's degree at some point. Some colleges and universities will review and accept some of your military training for college credit. It might save you from taking a class or two somewhere along the line.

Service Branch	Request Transcript From
U.S. Army	https://aartstranscript.leavenworth.army.mil
U.S. Navy	http://smart.cnet.navy.mil
U.S. Marine Corps	http://smart.cnet.navy.mil

| U.S. Air Force | www.au.af.mil/ccaf |
| U.S. Coast Guard | www.uscg.mil/hq/capemay/degree.htm |

Health and Life Insurance

Medical costs are an ever-increasing fact of life. If you are being involuntarily separated under other than adverse conditions, you may be eligible for an extension of your health benefits as you transition from the military.

How long an extension you may receive depends upon how long you have been in the service and upon the conditions of your separation. For example, certain service members being involuntarily separated with other than adverse conditions and having served less than six years of duty could receive 60 days of additional military medical coverage; those with over six years could receive 120 days of extended health benefits. At the end of the 60- or 120-day periods, there may also be the option of purchasing extended transitional health care insurance. In this case, you would have 60 days after your initial transitional health care ends to purchase the Continued Health Care Benefit Program (CHCBP).

If you are retiring, you must make it a point to meet with your health benefits advisor to review your available options for continued care. One possible option available to all separating service members is to purchase CHCBP, a medical coverage plan for three-month time periods, for up to 18 months. Ka-ching! We're talking expensive here, but one bad day that sees you in a hospital can cost even more.

Another issue to consider is your Servicemembers' Group Life Insurance (SGLI). The government will pay for an additional 120 days of life insurance coverage after you separate, whether you are retiring or not. This provides you with a bumper of time to decide whether you wish to convert all or part of your SGLI in $10K increments to something called Veterans' Group Life Insurance (VGLI).

VGLI is a five-year term insurance policy. That means that as you age, your cost to participate increases. At the end of five years, if you decide you no longer wish to have VGLI, you may convert it to a civilian life insurance policy. In most cases, the VA will send you notification within 30 days after you separate that you must make a decision regarding this benefit. If you want to be proactive, download the form from the VA's Web site (www.va.gov) or call them at 1-800-827-1000.

There are several other important notes to keep in mind concerning medical and dental topics:

- **Get a physical before you separate.** If you are retiring, you will be required to do so within four months of your retirement. If you are getting out as a result of a medical condition or if you are being involuntarily separated under certain chapter actions, you will be required to have a physical as well. If you have any questions regarding your requirements in this area, contact your Legal Office for clarification. All others should go ahead and get a physical even though it is not required. It is free health care and you and your family should take advantage of it while you can.

- **Get copies of your medical and dental records and those of your family.** Military medical records (yours and your family's) will remain government property even when you are no longer wearing a uniform. You will want to have a good copy or two of your records for your next physician to have as a medical history. If you are applying for VA disability benefits, you will also need to provide the VA with a copy of your medical file.

- **Get your pearly whites examined and cleaned within 90 days of separating from the military.** If you do not do this, be sure the dental clinic representative notes such in your dental records before you clear the facility. The VA will allow for a one-time exam and cleaning up to 90 days after your separation from the military, assuming you didn't do so beforehand.

- Make it a point to visit the medical board liaison officer at your servicing medical treatment facility if you believe you have a serious medical problem or service-related handicap.

Finances

Money, money, money. This is certainly an important and timely topic, isn't it? There are so many things to address on this subject that it's difficult to know where to begin. Let's try, however. Several big questions to ask yourself are

- Do I have enough money saved to transition out of the military? A careful review of your expenses and income are in order at this point. Create a budget if you haven't already done so, and be frugal with your cash. Like everything else, there will be a multitude of seen and unforeseen expenses. If you are having problems determining where you stand in your checkbook, consult the experts at the Family Service Center nearest you for assistance.

- What happens to the money in my Thrift Savings Plan (TSP) account? Your TSP is a defined-contribution retirement and investment plan that offers savings and tax benefits. Make sure you know how to manage this account as you change employers. You may incur penalties if it is not correctly managed.

- Am I eligible for any additional separation pay? Chances are, if you are being honorably but involuntarily separated and have served six years on active duty, you will have something coming your way. Your transition office will be able to answer this for you for certain. Generally speaking, separation pay (which is taxable, by the way) is authorized only if the following applies:

  - ☐ You have finished your first term of enlistment or period of obligated service, *and*

  - ☐ You have at least six years of service, *and*

  - ☐ You are separating involuntarily, *and*

- ☐ You are not yet eligible for retirement, *and*

- ☐ Your discharge is fully honorable

Separation pay is computed on the basis of 10 percent of your yearly base pay when you separate, multiplied by the number of years of active duty service you have.

- **Am I eligible for unemployment?** You might also be eligible for unemployment compensation after you separate from the military, if you are not immediately employed. This benefit is commonly referred to as Unemployment Compensation for Military Personnel (UCX). Eligibility for this benefit depends upon the state paying the claim. To meet the requirements for UCX, you must

  - ☐ Have been discharged or released under honorable conditions

  - ☐ Have been discharged or released after completing your first full term of active service to which you initially agreed to service, *or*

  - ☐ Have been discharged or released from the government under an early release program because of a medical disqualification, pregnancy, parenthood, or a service-incurred injury or disability. Other qualifying situations include personality disorder or ineptitude, but only if the service was continuous for 365 days or more.

  Reservists who have completed 90 consecutive days of active duty service may also have their military service and wages assigned for the purpose of determining entitlement of UCX, provided you were discharged under honorable conditions.

- **How will my retirement pay be calculated?** If you entered the service after July 31, 1986, you will be given a choice of retirement plans at your fifteenth year of service. Log on to www.dod.mil/militarypay for further guidance in this area. Another good Web site for guidance with retired pay is www.dfas.mil/money/retired/index.htm. The bottom line is this: Connect with your transition office and/or your Retirement Services Office to determine your eligibility for such pay and with your Finance Office to ensure that your updated address and banking information is on file.

- **If retiring and I elect SBP, how much will it cost me?** This answer will depend on which level of coverage you choose. Visit your installation's Retirement Services Office or your transition office for more information. Military-related associations may also be able to provide you with objective information on the topic.

- **Do I know what salary range to aim for in my job search?** This is another important reason to have a grip on your finances. Chapter 8, "Evaluating and Negotiating Job Offers," will offer you more insight on this topic.

- **What other types of financial assistance (such as VA and SBA loans) might be available to me?** Accessing sites online such as www.va.gov and www.sba.gov can give you lots of information about various types of assistance.

- **Does the Finance Office have my forwarding address so I can receive my W2 form next year?** Simply check with your Finance Office to ensure that they have the correct address.

- **What is my credit rating with the three major credit reporting bureaus?** Get a copy of your credit report to make sure everything is in order. Here is the contact information for the three major agencies:

   □ Experian, P.O. Box 2104, Allen, TX 75013-2104, toll free 1-888-397-3742 or online at www.experian.com/product/consumer.

   □ Equifax, P.O. Box 105873, Atlanta, GA 30348, toll free 1-800-685-1111 or online at www.equifax.com.

□ Trans Union Corp, P.O. Box 390, Springfield, PA
19064-0390, toll free at 1-800-916-8800 or online at
www.tuc.com.

If you live in specific states (such as Georgia, Maryland,
Massachusetts, and Vermont) you may be eligible for a free
credit report on a yearly basis. Check the Web site for specifics.
Also, if you want to limit who can request your personal information, contact the agencies and tell them that no one can access
it without your expressed permission. This may cut down on
junk mail and unwanted intrusions into your personal financial
information.

Protect Yourself from Identify Theft

In the military, you are often known simply by your Social Security
number. If you are married to a military service member, you
may not even remember your own number anymore as you are
always required to give your spouse's for everything. Now more
than ever, it is important to safeguard this all too freely given
information.

□ Guard your Social Security number at all times. Avoid having it pre-printed on your personal checks, and always
shred documents having it listed once you no longer
need them.

□ Never give your Social Security number or any personal
information to anyone on the telephone unless you have
made the call and know where it is you are calling in the
first place.

□ Install a firewall on your personal computer if you have
Internet access.

□ Review your credit reports at least once a year to make
sure there are no discrepancies.

□ Make sure your mailbox is secure and that mail (having
your Social Security number on it) can't be easily
removed.

Reserve Affiliation

Retirees need not apply. Everyone else, except for certain chapter actions, must visit the reserve component career counselor. If you have not served eight years in the military, you may be required to do so in a reserve capacity with a reserve or National Guard unit or with the individual ready reserves. Affiliation with a reserve or Guard unit has its benefits. Some of them include extra cash, benefits, and promotion. You eventually get to retire with them if you choose to and you might get the opportunity to continue your travel to foreign and exotic places.

Disabled Veterans

The Veterans Administration will play a vital role in your and your family's post military life. Chapter 3, "VA Benefits and Other Opportunities," will delve into this topic in more detail. Suffice it to say here that you probably have a number of potential benefits and entitlements available to you through the VA.

You need to be sure that you attend a VA briefing before you separate from the service. If one is not available in your area, go online to the VA Web site (www.va.gov) and read the Benefits section carefully. Even if you attend a briefing, everything is in black and white on the Web site.

Of particular concern here will be your possible disability benefits. The VA believes that you entered the service in perfect health. If you exit the service in less than perfect health, you should be compensated for that difference. Translated, this means that you should apply for such benefits as you transition from the military. Even if you think you are not due any, apply for them. If you receive a 0% disability rating, then you've established a baseline in the event that future illnesses or other disabilities rear their ugly heads. You can't see into a crystal ball, and future mishaps you experience might have origins in your past military life.

Another plus: Disability monies are not taxed after a certain percentage. If you are retiring, your retirement pay may be offset by any disability compensation you receive. (The disability portion, however, will not be taxed, whereas your retirement pay might be affected. The exception to this at the time of this printing involves those having a disability rating of 50 percent or higher.)

Another benefit to applying for your disability benefit as you transition: Your medical records can go directly to the VA rather than to the huge record storage place in St. Louis, Missouri. This means that you don't waste precious time in the future having the VA request your records from St. Louis to begin your records review. The VA will already have them.

Disability monies may or may not mean a lot to you at this point in your life. After all, you are in your earning prime, right? You won't always be, however, and this source of income in later years might be beneficial to you. If you are honestly due it, take it. Installation procedures for applying as you transition may certainly differ from post to base. Ask the specialists at the transition center how you should go about submitting your claim as you transition from your own installation and branch of service.

In addition to disability compensation, there are other benefits such as VA home loans, educational benefits, and, as previously introduced, VGLI. These, along with others, will be discussed in more detail in Chapter 3, "VA Benefits and Other Opportunities."

The VA also sponsors a unique rehabilitation program called the Disabled Transition Assistance Program. Your local VA representative or your transition assistance office can point you in the right direction if you're interested in this program.

Individualized Transition Plan (ITP)

As mentioned earlier in this chapter, the DD 2648, is a required form that becomes a part of your official personnel file. Public Law 107-103 states that all exiting service members be informed regarding their potential benefits and entitlements. Completion of this form fulfills that legal requirement. After learning about your potential benefits and entitlements, you and your spouse, if applicable, are further entitled to receive assistance in developing an Individualized Transition Plan (ITP). The purpose of an ITP is to identify educational, training, and employment objectives. It further aims to assist you in developing a plan to achieve those objectives.

Retiree Benefits

As you plan your eventual retirement, you should contact the installation's retirement services officer and/or the transition office, depending upon where you are stationed, to schedule any available pre-retirement briefings. A multitude of topics ranging from how to obtain your retiree ID card, to facility and service availability, to survivor benefit plan elections, will be discussed. Every issue is important, and you can't afford ignorance on any of the topics.

Leaving the Service: Important Points to Remember

As you plan to leave the service, don't forget about the following:

Your DD 214

Everyone who leaves the military receives a DD 214, Certificate of Release or Discharge from Active Duty. This is an incredibly important document for which you must always maintain accountability.

Before you sign your DD 214, be sure it is 100 percent accurate. If you haven't already done so by now, assemble, in chronological order, all your certificates of training and military orders into one binder. When you review your draft DD 214, make sure everything (such as your education and awards) is included on it.

Once you sign this form, it is final. It documents your entire military existence and will be an important form later for such uses as when you try to use your VA benefits, obtain a federal job, vote, or obtain federal financial aid. It would be to your advantage to keep your original in a safe place, such as a safe deposit box. You may want to consider registering it at your local county courthouse. If you ever lose the document, you can easily obtain a copy there.

Military Records

You'll want to take special care of your military records.

- Make sure all your military records are in good order. It may be a hassle to review them and get any inconsistencies or errors corrected now. It will, however, be easier now than later. It may truly matter at some point in your life. If you do find an error in your records at some point, you'll be required to provide a written request to correct the error within three years of its discovery.

- The National Personnel Records Center can assist you in the event that you lose or misplace any medals or ribbons you wish to keep. Also, if you feel as though you should have received a particular medal or ribbon and did not, they will research the matter for you. They can be contacted at The National Personnel Records Center, Attention: Military Personnel Records, 9700 Page Boulevard, St. Louis, MO 63132-5000.

Discharge Decisions

If you feel you are being discharged from the military unfairly, you can request a review of your situation. Each of the services has its own discharge review boards who in turn have the authority to change or correct any discharge or dismissal from the service. The board, however, has no authority to address medical or general court martial discharges. You, your next of kin, or legal representative have 15 years from the time of your discharge to make such an inquiry using a DD Form 293, Application for Review of Discharge or Separation from the Armed Forces.

Miscellaneous

If your transition involves relocating...

- Be sure you provide change-of-address cards to your post office.

- Wherever you end up calling home, be sure you register to vote by contacting the county voting clerk.

At Your Final Out-Processing

Procedures will of course vary from post to base. Usually, you can expect to receive your military clearing papers within 10 duty days of your availability date or active separation if not taking transition leave or permissive travel (TDY/TAD). Once you receive these, you'll be tasked with getting the "good to go" check mark from a number of facilities and service providers. You have to hit the pavement now! If you don't know the hours of operation for the places you have to go to, call in advance. Save yourself the headache of having to make return trips.

You will be required to present your completed clearing papers at your final out-processing. You may have to present the following as well:

- Your updated ID card (keep in mind that the expiration date on your ID card must match the separation date on your orders).

- Your original medical and dental records (be sure you have already made your personal copies and copies for the VA).

- The result of your completed physical exam if you are retiring (this is usually a time-sensitive task, meaning that you must complete the exam not earlier than four months prior to your transition leave date but no later than one month before your retirement).

- DD 2648 (ITP), which proves that you received your mandatory preseparation counseling.

- DD Form 2656, Survivor Benefit Plan election. This is required only if you are retiring. (Your spouse, if you have one, will be required to have signed this form if you have elected not to take this coverage.)

- VA Form 21-526, the claim for a VA disability rating.

- If you are stationed overseas and wish to remain there after your separation, then you will also have to show proof that you have applied for and received command approval to do so. Country laws regarding this topic vary. Check with your legal services for details concerning your situation.

Focus on the Family

According to a 2001 survey (2001 Demographics Report, compiled from multiple sources by the Military Family Resource Center), there are over 1,369,167 active duty service members. Nearly 52 percent of these service members are married. Forgive me for stating the obvious, but leaving the military really is a big deal that not only affects you but your family, if you are so blessed.

CHAPTER 3 VA Benefits and Other Opportunities

If your service in the U.S. military can be characterized as "honorable," then you may be eligible for a whole host of benefits and entitlements offered by the Veterans Administration.

Veterans Benefits: A Closer Look

In your post military life, the Veterans Administration will play a large role in the facilitation of various benefits and entitlements that may be due you upon your separation from the service. To investigate or apply for these benefits, contact any VA office by calling toll free 1-800-827-1000. You can also visit the VA Web site at www.va.gov to learn everything you've ever wanted to know about them and more. You are now able to download most of the required forms to apply for benefits.

Please note that I've made every effort here, as throughout this book, to provide you with the most accurate and up-to-date information concerning the subject at hand. As in life, however, the rules, regulations, eligibility criteria, and availability are subject to change. Always check with the VA directly for the most current information.

Simply put, the VA is your connection to your benefits from serving in the military after you leave active duty service. Eligibility for most VA benefits is based upon discharge from active military service under other than dishonorable conditions. Some military personnel may even be eligible for certain VA benefits while on active duty when they have completed 90 days of service during wartime or conflict periods or 2 years of military service since 1980 or 181 days during peacetime. As a veteran, you have a myriad of potential benefits, and you owe it to yourself to examine them all.

To get into the VA system for the first time after release from active duty, you must send a copy of your DD 214 along with your application for benefits. You can file your application and discharge papers with any VA regional office.

Specifically, you should investigate your benefits as they relate to

- Education and training
- Life insurance
- Home loans
- Disability compensation and pension
- Vocational rehabilitation and employment
- Health care
- Family and survivors
- Burial

Education and Training Benefits

To stay competitive in today's job market, you must commit yourself to continuing education and training. The VA pays monthly benefits to eligible veterans, dependents, reservists, and service members, which can help finance their education. You can use your benefits for the following:

- Undergraduate study at a college or university
- Graduate study at a college or university
- Technical or vocational training
- Correspondence and flight training

You might also be able to qualify for a work-study allowance.

Depending upon when you entered the service, you may have already paid into an education program, be it the GI Bill, Active Duty, Chapter 30; the Veterans Educational Assistance Program (VEAP), Chapter 32; or the GI Bill, Selective Reserve, Chapter 1606. For the first two programs listed, you have 10 years from your release date to use the benefits. Limited extensions may be available. For the last program listed, you also have 10 years from the date of eligibility for the program, or until you are released from the Selected Reserve or National Guard. You have 14 years to use these benefits if your eligibility began on or after October 1, 1992. If you were activated under Title 10, your period of eligibility is extended by your time on active duty plus four months. You may be eligible for separate extensions for each activation. Extensions are not available if you were activated under Title 32.

The Way It Was

She said: At that time [when he transitioned out of the military], we had to find out for ourselves what we were entitled to for the most part.

—Sherry Martin, Office Manager, Resource Consultants, Inc.

He said: I didn't retire, so a lot of the benefits and entitlements didn't apply to me. It was nice to be the ruler of my own life instead of at the beck and call of people that may not have had my best interest at heart. We had a plan and money, but didn't realize how fast it goes.

—Steve Martin, Technical Instructor, General Dynamics

Life Insurance Benefits

There are a few options available in this area, depending upon whether you are active duty or not. We will focus here on the options relevant to veterans or those soon to be.

Servicemembers' Group Life Insurance (SGLI) is a low-cost life insurance available to service members and reservists upon active duty. When you decide to leave the military, you will have 120 days of continued SGLI coverage from the date of your effective out. This gives you time to consider whether you want convert your SGLI to Veterans' Group Life Insurance (VGLI). VGLI is a five-year term insurance policy. At the end of five years, you may either renew it or convert it to a civilian policy in $10,000 increments. As with all term insurance, you will find that the older you get, the more expensive this insurance becomes. You must complete conversion to a commercial policy with the "no health questions asked" benefit within 120 days of separation from either active duty or the reserves.

Service-Disabled Veterans' Insurance (RH Insurance) is a policy having a basic $10,000 coverage. You must apply within two years from the date of notification of your service-connected disability to receive this benefit. A $20,000 supplementary policy is available if premium payments for the basic policy are waived due to total disability. For this benefit, you must apply within one year of approval of waiver of your premiums.

Finally, there is Veterans' Mortgage Life Insurance (VMLI). This benefit is actually a mortgage protection insurance issued to those who are severely disabled who have also received grants for Specially Adapted Housing from the VA. Maximum coverage under this plan is $90,000, and veterans must apply for the plan before the age of 70.

Home Loan Benefits

The VA will also assist you in your home ownership aspirations. Veterans with qualifying service are eligible for VA home loan services including guaranteed loans for the purchase of a home, a manufactured home, a manufactured home and lot, and certain types of condominiums.

The VA also offers guaranteed loans for the building, repairing, and improving of homes. You may also be able to use this benefit to refinance an existing home loan. Note that "guarantee" does not mean "the VA actually loans you the money." You are still responsible for finding a lender. The VA merely guarantees the repayment of that loan up to a certain point if the borrower fails to repay the loan.

No down payment is required for most home loans. You must obtain a certificate of eligibility from the VA before you can claim such a benefit. Depending upon the nature of your disability, you may also receive grants to have your home specially adapted to your exact needs.

If you are a Native American living on Trust Land, then you may qualify for a direct home loan. There is no time limit for taking advantage of this benefit. If you have filed a claim for disability compensation with the VA, they may in turn waive the funding fee required for use of this benefit.

Disability Compensation and Pension Benefits

As mentioned in Chapter 2, the VA believes that when you joined the military you did so in perfect health. If you leave in less than perfect health, the VA believes you should be compensated for it. The VA will compensate you on a monthly basis for disabilities incurred or aggravated during your time in service. You are not required to pay state or federal income on any disability money you receive. Your entitlement is established from the date of separation if the claim is filed within one year from separation.

As was pointed out in Chapter 2, be sure to apply for these benefits as you transition out of the service. It makes perfect sense and it could save you a lot of time in the future.

If you're retiring, remember that your military pay is reduced by any VA compensation received. There are exceptions to this policy. Enacted in November 2003, the National Defense Authorization Act called for concurrent receipt of military retired pay and VA disability pay for retirees with than 20 years of service and a disability rating of 50 percent or more. Perhaps other categories of disability percentages will likewise be affected in the future. That is unclear at this point. Keep informed of new legislation on this subject by periodically visiting the VA's Web site. Income that you may have received from Special Separation Benefits (SSB) and Voluntary Separation Incentives (VSI) may also affect the amount of VA compensation actually paid. There is no time limit for applying for this benefit, but you must have been discharged under other than dishonorable conditions.

The VA will pay you anywhere from $104 to $2,193 per month, depending upon your level of disability. You may be paid additional amounts if you are severely disabled or have lost a limb; you have a spouse, child (children), or dependent parent(s); or if you have a seriously disabled spouse. To apply for this benefit, complete VA Form 21-526, Veterans' Application for Compensation or Pension. You may apply online at http://vabenefits.vba.va.gov/vonapp. There are a number of benefits related to this one, including the following:

- Priority Medical Care

- Clothing Allowance

- Grants for Specially Adapted Housing

- Federal Employment Preference

- Military Exchange and Commissary Privileges

- Vocational Rehabilitation

- Service-Disabled Veterans' Insurance

- Automobile Grant and Adaptive Equipment

- State/Local Veterans' Benefits

Disability Pension
The disability pension is an income-based benefit that is paid to veterans with honorable wartime service who are permanently and totally disabled due to nonservice-connection disability (or who are 65 years or older). Again, there is no time limit imposed on you to apply for this benefit.

Vocational Rehabilitation and Employment Benefits

Veterans having a serious service-connected disability are afforded such services as vocational and personal counseling, education and training, financial aid, job assistance, and, if needed, medical and dental treatment. The goal of this program is to help eligible disabled veterans get and keep lasting and suitable employment. Eligibility is based on the following:

- You must first be awarded a monthly VA disability compensation payment. (In some cases, this requirement is waived.)

- You must have served on or after September 15, 1940, *and*

- Your service-connected disabilities must be rated at least a 20 percent by the VA, *and*

- You require the services to overcome an employment handicap, *and*

- It has been less than 12 years since the VA notified you of your eligibility.

The VA will pay for any training costs and special services you may require. While in training, the VA will also pay you a subsistence allowance. To apply for this benefit, complete VA Form 28-1900, Disabled Veterans' Application for Vocational Rehabilitation. You can also apply online at http://vabenefits.vba.va.gov/vonapp.

Health Care Benefits

The VA provides an extensive range of health care services to veterans, but you must be enrolled in this system to receive care. (Service-connected veterans are eligible for treatment of their service-connected disability even if they have not enrolled.) Such services include the following:

- Primary and specialty care

- Preventive medicine services

- Surgery

- Emergency care

- Drugs and pharmaceuticals

- Mental health and substance abuse treatment

- Nursing home/long-term care

- Home health care

- Respite and hospice care

- Homeless veterans' programs

- Veterans' centers

- Sexual trauma counseling and treatment

- Women's Veterans' Health Programs

Call 1-877-222-VETS to learn about all health benefits.

Combat veterans may receive free health care for up to two years from release of active duty for any illness possibly associated with service against a hostile force in war after the Gulf War or during a period of hostility after November 1, 1998.

Family and Survivor Benefits

Some family members of disabled or deceased veterans are eligible for benefits such as the following:

- Educational benefits

- Home loan guaranty for surviving spouse

- Medical care for family and survivors (CHAMPVA)

- Death pension

- Burial of spouse and eligible family members

- Dependency and Indemnity Compensation

Dependency and Indemnity Compensation (DIC) is a monthly benefit paid to eligible survivors of a military member who died while on active duty or a veteran whose death resulted from a service-related injury or disease. There are other instances where this benefit may apply to veterans whose death resulted from a non-service related injury or disease. Consult a VA representative for more information.

The basic rate of pay for DIC is $948 for eligible surviving spouses. In some cases, the VA may pay more.

To apply for this benefit, complete VA Form 21-534, Application for Dependency and Indemnity Compensation, Death Pension and Accrued Benefits by a Surviving Spouse or Child.

Burial Benefits

As a veteran, you and your eligible family members may be buried in a VA National Cemetery. This benefit includes the gravesite, the headstone or marker, opening and closing of the grave, and grounds maintenance. VA National Cemeteries are maintained as national shrines. Your surviving spouse or family member will be provided with a presidential memorial certificate and a burial flag.

Other Benefits

As a veteran, you may be eligible for the following benefits as well:

- State veterans' homes

- Homeless veterans' programs

- Civil Service Preference

- Overseas benefits

- Free state benefits such as

  □ Camping

  □ Hunting and fishing licenses

  □ Disabled veteran automobile license plates

  □ Boat trailer registration fees and taxes

  □ Handicapped parking card

☐ Watercraft registration

☐ Tuition for family members for some state colleges and universities

Additionally, Veterans Service Organizations (VSOs) and other organizations that have partnered with them can assist you with your VA benefits and your transition to civilian life.

Job Training Opportunities

As you make your transition from the military to the civilian world, take advantage of all services and opportunities that may be available to you. In addition to those offered by the military and the VA, the following options may interest you.

Workforce Investment Act

The Federal Workforce Investment Act (WIA) provides training and job search assistance. Individual states manage their own programs, but funding is provided by the federal government. If you are leaving the military and do not have a service-connected disability, contact your state employment services office to inquire about program eligibility and application procedures. If you are leaving the military with a disability, you may be eligible for other job training opportunities as well. Detailed information about WIA can be found on your state's Web page on the Internet.

Licensing and Certification Information

Certain occupations require a license or certificate. You may have done the same job in the military, but on the outside, you need a piece of paper to say that you're qualified to do it. Visit the Use Your Military Experience & Training (UMET) Web site to compare what you've done with what is required on the outside. Another Web site that may be helpful is Credentialing

Opportunities On-Line (COOL) at www.armyeducation.mil/cool.

Entrepreneurship: When You Want to Be Your Own Boss

Self-employment isn't for everyone, but it may be for you. If you have a healthy dose of realism mixed in with a dream or two and topped off with basic know-how and talent, you might very well be the right person to make a go of it.

People who are self-employed often find themselves working longer and harder than their 9–5 counterparts. The cost of starting your business, depending upon the nature of your venture, can be expensive. Many would-be entrepreneurs opt to begin their businesses on the side as they continue the drudgery of their full-time job. Businesses generally won't see a profit for at least six months to a year or even longer. Only you can decide which path is the best for you and your family.

To assist in researching this area, there are a number of resources available to you, not the least of which is the Small Business Administration (SBA). The SBA can be reached at 1-800-827-5722 or found online at www.sba.gov. With their resources, you can begin to make educated decisions, prepare a business plan, secure funding, and launch your business.

It would also be to your benefit to tap into your own network of contacts and to select a special mentor just for this process. A group of retired business executives who do just that can be located at www.score.org.

You can't go wrong by joining your local chamber of commerce, either. After all, the business of a chamber is to attract business. You will expand your professional database and potential customer base by untold numbers.

Focus on the Family

You may not have actually worn the uniform, but you have dearly paid the price of service nevertheless. You are a wife, a husband, or a child of a service member, and as such, you may be extended the opportunity to benefit from various entitlements, depending upon individual circumstances. Don't make the assumption that you are or are not eligible for the same benefits as your uniformed loved one. Always get the facts directly from the source of the potential opportunity.

CHAPTER 4 Job Search Necessities

Finding your next job is more than doable if you take the time to think about the process before you begin it. The simple acts of separating fact from fiction and implementing effective job search strategies will ensure your success.

A unique opportunity faces you as you transition out of the military. It's the opportunity to do anything you'd like to do with your career, and indeed with your life. You can choose to stay in your current career path or you can boldly go where you have never gone before. While the task in front of you might appear daunting at times, it is manageable. It may be new territory for you, but it is territory that won't be unfamiliar for long.

If there is one thing that will serve you well in the civilian world, it is the skill of being able to search for and find a job. The latest statistics suggest that people change jobs on average at least five to six times during the course of their careers.

You might not have a clue where to begin, or you might already know what you have to do. If you fall into the latter category, consider yourself in front of the proverbial power curve. In either case, it is to your benefit to review and/or learn the techniques and strategies typically used to conduct a job search. It's a bit like having the ability to speak a foreign language. Unless you use it, you often lose it. Besides, you never know when you will learn something new or revisit something old that makes all the difference in your efforts to find suitable and satisfying employment.

Job Search Myths and Realities

Everyone in the military knows someone who knows someone else who left behind the paltry uniformed pay scale for greener pastures and a six-figure salary. In most cases, this is a myth. In fact, there are several myths that seem to perpetuate themselves. To make realistic and educated decisions about your future, you should know what the myths—and the realities—are.

Myth: You will make more money on the outside.

Reality: Yes and no. There are a number of variables to consider here, including your particular career field and your level of expertise within that area. Supply and demand of a skill set, as well as geography, also plays a significant role. The only way to separate fact from fiction in this case is to do your own research and run the numbers. You might be surprised at your findings.

Myth: You need to find the perfect job when you get out of the military.

Reality: Chances are you won't find the perfect job *ever*. Perfect jobs don't exist. If you're lucky, you will find a job or continue in a career that provides you with professional and personal fulfillment most of the time. Don't make the mistake of glorifying life out of the uniform. Unless you become a slave to your own business, you will still have to report to someone else and maneuver the finer points of organizational politics.

Myth: Once you get hired by an employer, you're stuck.

Reality: You're never stuck. You can always get another job. That's one crystal-clear plus of being a civilian. You never have to wait for your service branch to cut your orders, telling you to move somewhere you don't want to go.

Myth: You will lose all job security once you leave the military.

Reality: There is no denying that the military offers a level of job security that is pretty difficult to match. Paychecks come on a regular basis. Benefits are generally readily available. Service members and their families are usually well taken care of in those areas. In the civilian world, the concept of job security is an illusion that everyone accepts. Paydays may come only once a month. Benefits may cost you a chunk of change out of that paycheck. You might show up at work one morning and find yourself unemployed that same afternoon. Of course, there are jobs and companies that appear to be more secure than others.

The truth is, however, that nothing is a sure thing forever—even in the military. The best way around this obstacle is to develop your own security. You can do this in a number of ways. You can build up a healthy savings account. You can arrange some of your benefits so they are not tied to your employment as a prerequisite. You can make yourself as indispensable to your new employer as possible. And, of course, it never hurts to know how to find another job, should the worst case happen.

Get a Job

Getting a job is more than just a feeling you have to have a job, but making the company truly believe you know how your skills, abilities, past experience, and training will benefit the company.

—Chris Babich, career counselor who specializes in assisting veterans

Establishing a Starting Point

Before you begin passing around your resume, take out a blank sheet of paper and write the answers to these questions:

- Where you would like to live after you leave the military?

- What job would you realistically like to have?

- How much money do you need and want to earn?

After you answer them, prioritize them. What matters most to you? Location? If so, pull out a map and draw a circle around where you want to live and focus your search on that area. Perhaps location takes a back seat to the actual job. If this is the case, then certainly your options are greatly increased. Focus instead on what you have to offer versus what is available. Is money your driving force? If so, go for the bucks. Remember, though, that what constitutes a stellar salary in one geographical location doesn't necessarily hold true for another area. Always take into consideration that cost-of-living factor.

Is it possible to prioritize your desires and actually find a job that fulfills all three factors? Sure, but it's not likely. If you find that you are able to meet two of the three factors, consider yourself lucky.

Have your significant other, if applicable in your case, do the same exercise and then compare answers. You might find this to be either a real eye-opening exercise or a reaffirming one. If you find that your answers differ by a landslide, then you might want to discuss the questions on a more in-depth level with one another. Life will be much easier for everyone in the family if you are both on the same page. If there is no meeting of the minds here, then at least be prepared for an even more challenging transition. In any event, going through this drill will give you a starting point from which you can begin to structure your own job search campaign.

It's important to remember that you can change your answers along the way, if you find it necessary or desirable. Flexibility is a job search must, and it's to your professional and personal advantage to periodically re-evaluate your answers and revise them as necessary. Tunnel vision is not an asset here; realism is necessary.

Effective Job Search Strategies

Without question, those who have transitioned successfully before you have done so with a well-thought-out plan of attack. Others have done so on sheer luck. A combination of the two is unbeatable. The following strategies and exercises are certain to improve your probability for employment.

Think like an employer.

Employers obviously want to hire the best possible candidates for their positions. That means they want to have someone come on board who is qualified and willing to do the job and is able to fit in with others in the organization. Take a look at the following list of other much-sought-after characteristics:

- Solid decision-making skills

- Ability to learn

- Flexibility, adaptability, and persistence

- Effective verbal and written communication skills

- Assertiveness

- Professional networking skills

- Basic computer literacy

- Knowledge of company's history and goals

Do you possess any or all of the above characteristics? If so, keep them in mind as you will draw on them for use in your resume and during your interview. If you feel that you are lacking any of these valuable traits, take the initiative to develop them. You won't be sorry. They are basic and universal skills that employers often seek.

Organize your job search campaign.

You have probably heard the well-worn expression that looking for a job is a full-time job itself. There is no question that finding a job requires a great amount of time, patience, and perseverance. The ideal is that you devote 40 hours a week to your job search efforts. Reality doesn't always support that ideal, however. Chances are, you are still employed by Uncle Sam and you still have professional responsibilities that inhibit full devotion to your search. Rather than bemoan this point, work with it. The amount of time you spend looking for a job isn't nearly as important as the quality of time you spend on it.

Organizing your job search means that you identify the tasks you will need to accomplish to become employed. You will need to

- **Schedule your job search activities just as you would an appointment on your calendar.** Make sure to correctly note names, job titles, addresses, and contact numbers. You are likely to need this information throughout the process of developing your leads.

- **Keep track of your initial contacts with employers and any follow-ups.** Once the action starts happening, it can happen fast. You might find it helpful to make notes, on copies of your resumes and/or cover letters you send out, to remind yourself of who you spoke with regarding what position on what date. You could also use a worksheet to log the activity, such as the example provided on the following page. Do what works best for you, but keep track of names, telephone numbers, e-mail addresses, positions sought, and your efforts towards securing employment. Doing so will assist you in your follow-up efforts and in expanding your professional network.

- **Set timelines for yourself.** For example, don't just say that you will draft a resume. Say that you will give yourself three working days to do it. Establishing a self-imposed deadline increases the likelihood of specific task completion. If you complete a bunch of little tasks, they most certainly will add up to a great big one, and before you know it, you'll be hired.

- **Re-evaluate your direction and progress on a regular basis.** This is critical. You can't make good decisions using outdated information.

Beware, however. There is an inherent danger in organizing. Quite often, too much time is spent analyzing what needs to be done and not enough time is spent actually doing it.

Date	Company	Contact	Action Status	Remarks

Activity Log

Tap into available job assistance resources.

You're not on your own in this transition. There are a number of reputable resources, military and civilian, available to assist you in finding your next job.

- **Military Career Transition Centers.** These were discussed in more detail in Chapter 2. To locate the nearest one to you, go online to www.dodtransportal.org.

- **U.S. Department of Labor.** In addition to finding out about any unemployment benefits you may be eligible for, the employment office can refer you to employers for actual interviews, at no cost to you.

- **Military and professional associations.** By using your contacts within military and professional associations, you tap into the opportunity-rich world of the hidden job market. It is here where jobs are filled before they are even announced to the public. If you aren't a member of any such groups, consider the benefits of such membership today.

- **College and university placement services.** If you have been attending school or plan to in the future, the placement services of your school can offer you job search advice and access to their employment database.

- **Executive search firms.** There are many search firms out there, and they all want your business. If you decide to hire a "headhunter," be sure you understand your financial obligation to them in the event you obtain employment while under contract with them. Use of these services may or may not cost you. Read the fine print before you sign anything. You may be required to attend their job search prep workshops and then specially arranged job fairs where you meet with representatives from their client companies. Once you are hired by a company, your relationship with the headhunter usually ends.

- **Employment agencies.** Employment agencies can help you land short-term, long-term, and, in some cases, permanent assignments with companies. Again, use of their services may or may not cost you. There are many reputable "no fee" agencies ready, willing, and able to assist you. Generally, you are interviewed by a representative of the agency who will then refer and/or place you with other companies for a specific period of time. In such cases, you usually remain an employee of the agency and not of the company where you happen to be assigned. In other cases, you may be placed with a client company for a certain period of time, after which you may be hired directly by that company and relieved of your obligation to the employment agency.

Identify your work history, marketable skills, abilities, and experiences.

Before you can persuade an employer to hire you, you have to have a clear understanding of what it is you have to offer him or her. Furthermore, you have to be able to express those marketable attributes verbally and in writing. This involves closely examining your past work history, your marketable skills and abilities, and your personal work values.

- **Your work history.** You may be able to recite your work history chapter and verse. While that is admirable, it may be more beneficial at this point to write it down in the form of a Master Career Catalog (see following pages). It will help you lay the groundwork for developing your resume and provide you with detailed job application information for future use.

Master Career Catalog

Use this form to fully document your work history. Refer back to it as you develop your resume or as you complete job application forms.

I.   Personal Information

Fill in the following information as applicable. Think of this as information that may appear on your resume.

Name: _____

Present Address: _____

Future Address: _____

Telephone: _____ E-mail: _____

II.   Education and Training

List your academic education chronologically, beginning with the most recent. Include high school only if you graduated within the last five years.

College/University: _____

Dates Attended: _____

Area of Study: _____

Semester/Credit Hours Completed: _____

Degree Awarded (if applicable): _____

Remarks: _____

☐ ☐ ☐

College/University: _____

Dates Attended: _____

Area of Study: _____

Semester/Credit Hours Completed: _____

Degree Awarded (if applicable): _____

Remarks: _____

☐ ☐ ☐

College/University: _____

Dates Attended: _____

Area of Study: _____

Semester/Credit Hours Completed: _____

Degree Awarded (if applicable): _____

Remarks: _____

☐ ☐ ☐

High School: _____

Dates Attended: _____

Area of Study: _____

Semester/Credit Hours Completed: _____

Degree Awarded (if applicable): _____

Remarks: _____

□ □ □

List your completed military training chronologically, beginning with the most recent. Make a note to indicate if you graduated a course with honors.

Course Title	Sponsor	Dates Attended
_____	_____	_____
_____	_____	_____
_____	_____	_____
_____	_____	_____
_____	_____	_____
_____	_____	_____
_____	_____	_____
_____	_____	_____
_____	_____	_____
_____	_____	_____

III.   Work Experience

Chart your work history for the last 10 years, beginning with your most recent position.

Job Title: _____

Organization: _____

Address: _____

Dates: From _____ To _____

Supervisor: _____

Supervisor's Telephone: _____

E-mail: _____

Beginning Salary/Pay Grade: _____

Ending _____

(continued)

(continued)

Job Responsibilities:

_____

_____

_____

_____

_____

Job Accomplishments:

_____

_____

_____

_____

_____

☐ ☐ ☐

Job Title: _____

Organization: _____

Address: _____

Dates: From _____ To _____

Supervisor: _____

Supervisor's Telephone: _____

E-mail: _____

Beginning Salary/Pay Grade: _____

Ending _____

Job Responsibilities:

_____

_____

_____

_____

Job Accomplishments:

_____

_____

_____

_____

☐ ☐ ☐

Job Title: _____

Organization: _____

Address: _____

Dates: From _____ To _____

Supervisor: _____

Supervisor's Telephone: _____

E-mail: _____

Beginning Salary/Pay Grade: _____

Ending _____

Job Responsibilities:

_____

_____

_____

_____

_____

_____

Job Accomplishments:

_____

_____

_____

_____

_____

☐ ☐ ☐

Job Title: _____

Organization: _____

Address: _____

Dates: From _____ To _____

Supervisor: _____

Supervisor's Telephone: _____

E-mail: _____

Beginning Salary/Pay Grade: _____

Ending _____

Job Responsibilities:

_____

_____

(continued)

(continued)

_____

_____

_____

_____

Job Accomplishments:

_____

_____

_____

_____

_____

□ □ □

Job Title: _____

Organization: _____

Address: _____

Dates: From _____ To _____

Supervisor: _____

Supervisor's Telephone: _____

E-mail: _____

Beginning Salary/Pay Grade: _____

Ending _____

Job Responsibilities:

_____

_____

_____

_____

_____

_____

Job Accomplishments:

_____

_____

_____

_____

_____

□ □ □

IV. Potential References

Select individuals who can attest to your personal and professional integrity. Never use anyone's name without obtaining prior permission.

Name: _____ Job Title: _____

Organization: _____

Telephone Number: _____ E-mail: _____

Check all that apply:

Personal Reference _____ Professional _____

Comments: _____

_____

_____

_____

☐ ☐ ☐

Name: _____ Job Title: _____

Organization: _____

Telephone Number: _____ E-mail: _____

Check all that apply:

Personal Reference _____ Professional _____

Comments: _____

_____

_____

_____

☐ ☐ ☐

Name: _____ Job Title: _____

Organization: _____

Telephone Number: _____ E-mail: _____

Check all that apply:

Personal Reference _____ Professional _____

Comments: _____

_____

_____

_____

☐ ☐ ☐

(continued)

(continued)

V. Other Relevant Information

Security Clearance:

Yes: _____ Level: _____

No: _____

Foreign Languages:

_____

_____

_____

Computer Skills (include software in which you are proficient):

_____

_____

_____

_____

Hobbies/Interests:

_____

_____

_____

Memberships:

_____

_____

_____

Community Involvement:

_____

_____

_____

_____

Other Information:

_____

_____

_____

- **Your marketable skills and abilities.** Once you have charted your career history, you will be able to better see where your talents lie. If it helps, go back through what you have completed in your work history and circle the main words that identify your skills and abilities.

After you do that, carry it one step further by classifying each one as a self-management skill, a transferable skill, or a technical skill. You might also think of other skills you did not include in your history. List them as well.

My Technical Skills

Technical skills are specific skills that are required to accomplish a given task. For example, if you are a network satellite engineer, you require network satellite engineering to accomplish your job.

_____

_____

_____

_____

_____

_____

_____

My Functional or Transferable Skills

These are common skills that may be used in different jobs and industries such as customer service, teaching, or consulting.

_____

_____

_____

_____

_____

_____

My Self-Management Skills

These are skills that describe you as a person. For example, you might be dependable and hard-working.

_____

_____

_____

_____

_____

_____

_____

_____

- **Personal work values and desires.** Your work history and your skills are important factors to consider as you plan for your next job. Equally important to consider are your personal work values. What matters to you? How do you want this next phase in your life to play out? Do you see yourself ramping up or powering down? Perhaps you've worked in a stressful job for a long time and want to avoid that in your next position. In the military, you're generally told what you're going to do and where you're going to do it. You have more of a choice as a civilian. That may be an appealing idea to you, but it can also be overwhelming. Be kind to yourself and to your family. Carve out the time to examine what it is you want to achieve in this next life stage.

Something to Think About: Work Values That You May Already Value		
Salary	Job Satisfaction	Praise
Job Success	Location	Flexibility
Work Schedule	Advancement	Benefits
Power	Status	Challenge
Security	Work Environment	Affiliation
Recognition	Service to Others	Independence

Something to Think About: Life Values That You May Already Value		
Health	Wealth	Family
Prestige	Job Satisfaction	Travel
Creativity	Freedom	Trust
Learning	Responsibility	Religion
Control	End Results	Respect
Intimacy	Friends	Honesty
Fun	Stability	Popularity
Affiliation	Recognition	Competition
Living Conditions	Culture	Progression

Identify sources of employment opportunities.

Potential sources of employment can be found literally any-where. The job assistance resources mentioned earlier in this chapter provide information on job availability in addition to job search assistance. An extensive list of online resources is also provided to you in the appendix. The following sources should also be considered:

- **Hidden job market opportunities.** Networking is the deal. You will find out about more "hidden" job opportun-ities through casual conversation with well-connected friends and colleagues than you ever will by looking in the newspaper.

- **Job fairs.** If you attend a job fair, you may or may not walk away from it with an actual job. Chances are more the latter. What you will most certainly walk away with is information, and that is job search gold. Job fairs are a terrific place to meet people, gather business cards and company literature, and learn about real and projected opportunities. After the fair, your work begins in earnest. That is when you begin to tailor your resume to specific openings and write cover letters directly to individuals you met. Remember to track your activity!

- **Printed and online employment listings.** Job vacancies are advertised in printed form and in cyberspace in newspapers, trade journals, magazines, and on job boards. You won't have a problem finding job opportunities listed unless you are focusing your search on one tiny corner of the universe and refuse to look elsewhere. In which case, creativity might be a real requirement for your search. (See the appendix for more information regarding specific Web sites.)

- **Federal, state, and local offices.** According to the American Forces Information Service, hiring of military veterans across the federal civilian workforce in Fiscal Year 2002 increased by more than 19 percent from the previous year ("Federal Hiring of Nations' Military Veterans Increase," American Forces Information Service News Article, January 16, 2004). Federal employment opportunities may be located online at www.usajobs.opm.gov. Contact your local state and city offices (or their respective Web sites) for potential employment opportunities. (If you don't know the address, a good search engine such as Google.com or Yahoo.com should get you there in a couple of clicks.)

- **Industry directories.** Industry directories, available at your local library or online, can provide you with detailed information regarding a company's business, personnel, and financial stability.

- **Chambers of commerce.** Chambers are an excellent place to learn about businesses within the community. After all, their business is to attract business. Contact the chamber of commerce in the area you're interested in and inquire about a local employer listing. Usually these lists, along with new-comer welcome packets, can be purchased at a minimal price or are free.

Activate your network.

It may be cliché to say that it's not what you know, but who you know. Yet people you know and will know are your greatest asset in the job search process. Now is the time to activate your network. Everyone you know should know that you are looking for employment. Word of mouth is a productive tool in this process.

Networking is the act of developing and expanding your relationships with others. It is a continuous process that promotes a reciprocal exchange of information for the benefit of all parties. Your network is made stronger when you not only take from it, but also when you give back to it.

Tales from the Employed

Retire [or transition] from an area that you worked in while in the military so that you have made the necessary contacts. I retired on the East Coast and moved to a new town so it was difficult to network for a job.

—Laurie Davis, Independent Women's Health Care Consultant and U.S. Army Colonel (Ret.)

The best jobs are found by networking. Sometimes a position will even be created for you!

—Dale Michaels, Defense Contractor

I was approached for a job by a couple of civilians that I had previously worked with at the flight line.

—Thomas Wiederstein, Instructor, DOD Unmanned Aerial Vehicle (UAV) School

You can see from the comments of those above, and you probably know from your own experience, that networking is key to the success of your job search. Take a few minutes and jot down the names of those you already know who could be of assistance to you. Think about your friends, neighbors, relatives, past and present co-workers and supervisors, and fellow members in any professional, personal, or religious organization.

Select your references with care.

Employers often contact your references to ask them questions about you with regard to such areas as

- Length of employment
- Quality of work performed
- Level and scope of responsibility
- Interpersonal skills
- Timeliness (personal and professional)
- Reason for leaving previous employer
- Potential disqualifications from future employment

Make sure you choose and nurture your personal and professional references with care. You can have as many references as you like; however, three to five is generally adequate. Before you use anyone's name, obtain permission to do so. Ask your references what they would say about you if called upon. Coach them if necessary. Network with these individuals, too. Keep them informed about your job search status. Avoid overuse of any one person's name. Don't include their names on your resume. Create a separate document that lists each reference's

- Name
- Company and job title
- Address
- Telephone and e-mail
- Relationship to you

Network Contacts

Name	Company	Telephone	E-mail

Pitch yourself.

In your job search, you have to be able to confidently and intelligently talk about your skills, abilities, and qualifications. To this end, a two-minute sales pitch can be of great help and should contain the following:

- Relevant work experience

- Relevant skills or strengths

- Significant career accomplishments

- Applicable training or education

- A high-impact closing that clearly communicates your potential benefit to the company

You should prepare a short version and a longer version for use as the occasion demands. The goal here isn't to sound like a recording, however. Keep it natural and informative.

Be realistic and reasonable.

There will be days when it seems like everyone wants to hire you, and days when you just want to give up. Don't throw in the towel when the going gets rough. Accept the fact that finding a job doesn't usually happen overnight. You may want to be employed your first day as a civilian, but reality says that doesn't always happen. The average job search can take anywhere from three to six months. If you focus too much on the future and not enough on the day-to-day requirements for getting to your goal, you will become quickly overwhelmed. Keep it real. Keep it in the present with the occasional thought splurge to the future. Manage your job search. Don't let events manage you.

Focus on the Family

The skills discussed in this chapter are not just for those who've worn the uniform. While they are targeted to that audience, they are nevertheless based on universally practiced job search techniques and can be used by anyone who seeks employment— including you! A job search is a surprisingly personal process that demands great self-awareness and focused determination. Those characteristics, coupled with the knowledge of the practical job search strategies outlined in this chapter, will increase your chances for future career success.

CHAPTER 5 Building an Adaptable Resume

When you wear your military dress uniform, you are more or less a walking resume. Someone familiar with the insignia can easily determine about how long you've been in the military, which unit you're currently attached to, and where you've been stationed in the past. They know, without even asking, if you've jumped out of airplanes or if you can fire a weapon with any degree of skill.

In the civilian world of work, things are just not that transparent. You have to tell someone all about your skills and abilities. In the course of your job search, you will no doubt have many occasions to advertise the attributes you have to offer. This chapter will focus on the way you do this on paper: with your resume.

Why You Need a Resume

Before you begin to craft your resume, take a few moments to contemplate the reason behind it.

Potential employers may or may not know you personally. There might be an occasion when your resume is just a piece of paper to be filed in your new personnel folder. The employer already knows everything about you and wants to hire you based upon your past relationship with him or her. Awesome for you! You have presented yourself well, and the stress of creating and perfecting your resume may not concern you too much.

If, on the other hand, you are not automatically locked into a new job, you must somehow communicate your skills, abilities, credentials, and experiences on paper. You're about to create a critical document in your master plan, and you need to be sure that you take the time to do it right. Unfortunately, once you get it right, that won't be the end of it. As you apply for different opportunities, you will need to go back and revise your creation to better target the employer's desired and/or required qualifications. In other words, one size doesn't fit all. If you try to make it fit, you shortchange your chances for being hired.

There are several concepts to keep in mind as you begin this process. First, remember that you are not writing this resume for you. It only happens to be *about* you. It should be written for the employer. You'll want to get a second and third opinion on your resume after you've drafted it and before you hand it out to anyone. When you ask someone to look it over for you, try to select someone who is knowledgeable in your career field and who will be truthful, objective, and helpful.

Second, keep in mind that your resume, as powerful as it can be, more than likely won't land you a job. If it is well written and if you have the required skills and experiences that an employer is seeking, it may land you an interview, and that is the intent of writing it in the first place.

Finally, realize that there isn't one correct way to craft a resume. There are basic guidelines that the majority of job seekers follow and the majority of employers expect. Let your common sense, instinct, and research guide you as you go through this process. What works for others may not work for you.

Five Easy Steps for Designing Your Resume

You can always hire someone to write your resume for you. It's the easy, although often expensive, way to go. When you have someone else pen your resume for you, however, you run the risk of losing your unique voice in the document. A highly skilled writer, who knows you well or has a good feel for your communication style, might be able to capture this quality in your resume, although this is generally not the case.

You can spare your wallet the pain of such a purchase and develop a resume that truly represents who you are professionally in skills, experiences, and voice. I've provided a simple yet effective plan for showcasing your hard-earned qualifications.

The plan has five steps:

1. Step One: **Identify the focus for your resume.**

2. Step Two: **Identify the content and language for your resume.**

3. Step Three: **Select the best format to use.**

4. Step Four: **Identify optional categories and include as appropriate.**

5. Step Five: **Review, edit, and revise your resume as necessary.**

Step One: Identify the focus for your resume.

Consider the absurd factoid that employers generally give your resume a 20-second reading before they have subconsciously made their initial impression regarding it. Twenty seconds is not a lot of time to grab someone's attention, but it's what you must strive for anyway. Being concise, clear, and grammatically correct will help you to do just that. Your resume will stand a better chance if you clearly develop these three elements:

- The heading

- The objective

- The summary of your professional qualifications

The Heading

The heading is usually the first thing the employer looks at on your resume. It tells him or her who you are and how you can be contacted. If it is presented the wrong way, it can also tell the employer more about you than you might want him or her to know right off the bat.

Your name should be placed on the first line of the resume, followed by your address, a telephone number or two, and an e-mail address. You don't need to add more than that. Avoid using your military rank or newly achieved "Retired" label anywhere in your heading.

Avoid:	LTC James M. Michaels (Ret.)
Use:	Mr. James M. Michaels
	James M. Michaels

Exposing your rank right up front may backfire on you for two reasons. First, the civilian employer reading your resume may not have a clue what it means. Second, if the employer does understand what it means, he might interpret it as a point of self-inflated importance. If that offends you, accept my apology. The reality is this: When you're a civilian, you're a civilian. Your level of expertise is important, but expertise does not connote a particular rank or status in the civilian workplace.

It's also a good idea to omit any reference to being a retiree, if that applies to you. A retiree in the military is not the same thing as a retiree in the civilian world, where it might conjure images of being a senior citizen. You don't need to suggest that at this point in your job search.

If you have an academic degree and it is a requirement for the job you're designing your resume for, then it would be appropriate to tack it on behind your name.

Use:	Mr. James M. Michaels, M.Ed.

After your name, include your contact information. Sounds easy enough. With transitioning military personnel, however, it can become a complicated issue. For the ease of writing your resume, use your current mailing address. If you are stationed in one location and will be moving to another location and if you have an address where you can expect to receive mail there, you may want to use a split heading. A split heading is one that includes two addresses. For example:

John M. Michaels
john.michaels@myemail.com

Present:	After July 1st:
525 Catalina Drive	1414 Main Street
Sierra Vista, Arizona 00000	Tampa, Florida 00000
(555) 555-5555	(555) 555-5555

Notice a couple of things here. First, the name is bolded and uses a slightly larger font size than the e-mail address beneath it. By doing this, you place more emphasis on your name, which is what you're trying to get the employer to remember. In this example, the e-mail address is placed directly underneath the name, in a font that is one point smaller and italicized. The nice thing about your name and e-mail is that both of them stay the same, regardless of where you are physically located.

Whether or not you use a split heading approach will of course depend upon your immediate travel plans. If you are planning to stay in the same area, your heading could follow this format:

John M. Michaels
525 Catalina Drive
Sierra Vista, Arizona 00000
(555) 555-5555
john.michaels@myemail.com

The name is still bolded and typed in a larger font, giving it emphasis. The address and the e-mail follow, centered under the name.

If your resume is more than one page in length, it is not necessary to repeat the entire heading on the second page. Include your bolded name and indicate that it is page two. For example:

John M. Michaels   Page Two

or

John M. Michaels
Page Two

Remember, these are just examples of formatting. There are multiple ways that you can illustrate this information. The key is to strive for a professional appearance. Yet another cliché lives on: You don't get a second chance to make a first impression.

The Objective

Your resume should have a unifying theme. You are the topic. Your skills, experience, and talents are the guts of the work. You have to write your resume in such a way that you appear to know what you want to do, whether that's actually the case or not.

Resume writing experts argue whether you need to state an objective—a job title or description—on your resume. There are good reasons for and against; however, one fact is clear. Your resume must have an objective, whether you state it outright or not. With no objective, you lack focus. Without focus, you flounder. Every line on your resume should support your stated or unstated objective. If it doesn't, you should question whether that line belongs on your resume at all. The objective is *that* important.

If you want to stay in your present career field, coming up with an objective shouldn't be difficult. You can make it broad-based towards an industry or zoom in on a specific job with a specific company. For example:

> **Broad-based objective:** A managerial position within the telecommunications industry.

> **Specific objective:** Director of Operations for Your Great Company, Inc.

If you wish to switch career fields, then you need to be creative in writing your objective, depending upon your actual exposure to and experience in that desired field. If you're switching gears drastically, you'll need to make a concerted effort to market your transferable skills.

By including your objective on your resume, you give the employer a break by defining your wishes immediately.

Employers like that. This is good use of your 20 seconds! Don't include an objective if you're creating a resume for use in a job fair, where there may be multiple opportunities to consider, or if you're passing your resume off to a contact at a company that doesn't have a specific opening announced.

A clearly written objective can do wonders for your chances of obtaining an interview. Each time you apply for a different job, you need to be certain that your objective (whether you include it on your resume or not) matches the position for which you are applying.

The Summary of Your Professional Qualifications

Like the job objective, a summary of qualifications section can help your resume survive that initial scanning process. It gives the employer a quick synopsis of your experience and specialized expertise. It immediately shows him or her whether there is potential for a match between you and the job. Your summary should contain big-picture (yet targeted and relevant) information as it directly relates to the job you're applying for. Specifically, it might contain the following:

- The number of years of experience you have in your field

- Any specialized expertise or required credentials you may have

- Mention of your more outstanding management skills or technical abilities

Here is an example of a summary for a resume targeted towards law enforcement:

> Ten years of experience in the field of law enforcement with emphasis on management, crime prevention, criminal investigations, and patrol. Knowledgeable of federal, state, and local laws and ordinances. Excellent communication and investigative skills. Computer literate. Weapons qualified. Maintain a Department of Defense secret security clearance. Physically fit. Drug free. Received recognition on a number of occasions for superior police work.

Here is the same summary shown in a different layout:

- Ten years of law enforcement experience with emphasis on management, crime prevention, criminal investigations, and patrol.

- Knowledgeable of federal, state, and local laws and ordinances.

- Excellent communication and investigative skills.

- Computer literate.

- Weapons qualified.

- Maintain a Department of Defense secret security clearance.

- Physically fit and drug free.

- Received recognition on a number of occasions for superior police work.

Your summary should be just that—a summary. It should not take up half the page. Each time you apply for a different job, you should tailor this summary to the important skills sought by the employer for the job. It takes some effort to do this, but details count. Attention to detail will determine whether you get a job interview or a job itself—or not.

Step Two: Identify the content and language for your resume.

No doubt you have a lot of experience from which you can draw; however, you can't include all of it in one resume. Granted, if you have a number of years of experience, it can be difficult to decide what to include and what to omit. The key is to focus on what is most relevant. If it helps, ask yourself this question: *"Does this experience fully support my job objective for this resume?"* If the answer is yes, then include the experience. If the answer is no, leave it off. It's that easy.

You will have what will seem like a lifetime of stuff that won't be listed on your resume. Accept that and avoid changing the font size to three-point so that you can include everything you've ever done. Does your future employer really need to know you graduated with honors from the exclusive military action officer's writing course? Probably not.

Using the Right Lingo

In addition to deciding the content for your resume, you have to decide what type of language to use, military jargon or everyday English. If you're targeting a job within the defense industry, feel free to use the military jargon to which you've become accustomed. The defense industry likes to hire employees who understand the lingo. On the other hand, if you're targeting a job outside that arena, you may have to use everyday English. If you were to take someone who has never been exposed to life in the military and plant them in the middle of a typical conversation between service members discussing work, that person would probably feel as though he was a stranger in an even stranger land.

The military loves its acronyms. Once you get used to them, it's not so bad; however, civilian employers may not understand them at all. I've provided the following translations to assist you in crafting your resume and your speech. Note that some words or job titles may be clearly understood without changing them.

Common Translations

In the Military	In the Civilian World
Commander	Director/Senior Manager/President
Executive Officer	Deputy Director/Assistant
Action Officer	Senior Analyst
Branch or Division Chief	Branch/Division Chief
Program or Project Manager	Program or Project Manager

(continued)

(continued)

In the Military	In the Civilian World
General officers	President/Senior Director/ Chairperson
	Chief Executive Officer (CEO)
	Chief Operating Officer (COO)
	Chief Financial Officer (CFO)
	Senior Vice President
	Executive Vice President
Senior field grade officer	Senior Administrator/ Chief Executive
	Department head/ Program Director
	Deputy Chief/Senior Executive
Field grade officer	Executive/Manager
Company grade officers	Associate/Operations Officer
	Unit or Section Manager
Warrant officers	Director/Specialist/ Department Manager
Senior NCOs	Director/First-Line Supervisor
Infantry	Ground security force
Sergeant Major	Senior Advisor
First Sergeant	Personnel Manager
Squad Leader	Team Leader/Team Chief
Supply Sergeant	Supply Manager/Logistics Manager
Operations NCO	Operations Manager
NCO	Supervisor/Manager

In the Military	In the Civilian World
OER/NCOER	performance rating/evaluation
AI	additionally skilled in...
AAM-ARCOM	award/recognition
ANCOC/BNCOC	advanced (specialty) course
battalion (BN)	unit/organization/agency
headquarters	headquarters
combat	conflict/hostilities/emergency
	highly hazardous conditions
garrison	organization/company
company	company/unit/department
correspondence course	extension course/ distance learning
	correspondence course
leader	supervisor/manager
medal	award/recognition
military personnel office (MILPO)	personnel office
mission	task/function/objective
military occupation specialty (MOS)	career specialty
platoon	section/element/department
Platoon Sergeant	Supervisor/Instructor/Trainer
physical training (PT)	physical training
reconnaissance	data collection/survey/analysis
regulations	policy/guidelines/instructions

(continued)

(continued)

In the Military	In the Civilian World
security clearance	security clearance
soldiers/airmen/marines/ sailors	personnel/staff/ employees/ individuals/people
subordinates	employees/personnel/staff/ individuals/people
Temporary Duty (TDY)	business trip/temporary duty
Uniform Code of Military Justice (UCMJ)	legal action/document
TDA/MTOE	organizational structure/ human and material resources
Personnel Action Center (PAC)	personnel office
AR/DA/NAV Pamphlets	policy/guidelines/rules
team	team
squad	section
brigade	group/division
battalion	division
PLDC/BNCOC	leadership or advanced leadership development course
Command and General Staff College	Strategic Management Course
War College	Advanced Strategic Studies Course

It's important to write your resume in the language of the industry you are targeting. To help you better translate what you've done in the military into language that is easily understood by someone not familiar with the jargon, consult the O*NET OnLine Web site at the following address:

http://online.onetcenter.org

The O*NET is an extensive database of worker attributes and characteristics. It replaces the *Dictionary of Occupational Titles* as the source document for job-specific information. It is also a great tool that can help you capture the civilian essence of your ever-so-military job by using a crosswalk option on the main Web page.

The following steps walk you through the translation process, assuming that the Web page design hasn't changed since publication:

1. Access the main Web page at http://online.onetcenter.org.

2. Select the CROSSWALK option. (As of this printing, it is the third option after FIND OCCUPATIONS and SKILLS SEARCH.)

3. Enter your military occupation code in the correct box on the CROSSWALK SEARCH page. For example, if you entered 25A, Signal Officer or Warrant Officer, you would be taken to a screen that provides you with the O*NET number, civilian equivalent job title, and an option to select reports in either a summary, detailed, or customized format. The reports offer up the tasks, knowledges, skills, abilities, and work activities and context associated with Computer and Information System Managers (the civilian title for 25A). It also provides you with further detail regarding the level of preparation necessary to do the job, and characteristics and interests that tend to mesh well with a position in the field. Additionally, it gives you related occupations and links to the same type of information for those jobs. Finally, it offers you links to specific state wages and employment information, compliments of CareerInfoNet.

The idea here isn't to copy the information verbatim. What you can do, however, is read and analyze it for applicability in your own case. For example, notice the keywords that appear. Do those same keywords apply to your experience? What about the knowledges, skills, and abilities? Do any of them ring a bell in your camouflaged history? Maybe you called it something different in the military, but the basic job function is the same.

Resume Sentence Structure

If you're having flashbacks to English 101 courses, relax. Writing sentences for your resume is far easier than you might imagine. The key, as you might expect, is to consider your reading audience.

You should write your resume in such a way that the person reviewing it can understand what you have to offer in a clear and concise manner. Your statements should be accomplishment-based and should not read like an evaluation report or job description. You also have the benefit of omitting personal pronouns and freely using sentence fragments throughout your resume. Finally, your sentences should quantify your accomplishments, making your credentials action-based. Consider the following two examples:

Example 1: Managed a personnel division.

Example 2: Effectively managed a 100+ employee strong manpower and personnel division responsible for servicing Department of Defense employees throughout Europe.

Obviously, Example 2 gives more detail without going overboard. Here are several other examples:

- Successfully increased output by 35 percent in less than two months.

- Supervised the development and implementation of a self-directed training module.

- Effectively and efficiently managed a staff of 50 technicians working in a 24-hour telecommunications facility.

To get the attention of potential employers, your resume must contain words that communicate action. The following list of power words may help you to think of those that apply to your experiences.

Accounted	Acted	Adapted
Administered	Analyzed	Assessed
Budgeted	Built	Calculated
Classified	Coached	Compared
Conceptualized	Conducted	Consolidated
Consulted	Coordinated	Counseled
Created	Defined	Delegated
Designed	Developed	Directed
Edited	Eliminated	Established
Examined	Expanded	Facilitated
Generated	Guided	Headed
Identified	Implemented	Improved
Instructed	Investigated	Led
Maintained	Managed	Marketed
Mentored	Merged	Negotiated
Obtained	Operated	Organized
Performed	Planned	Presented
Projected	Provided	Published
Recognized	Recommended	Recorded
Reorganized	Repaired	Researched
Scheduled	Shaped	Simplified
Standardized	Streamlined	Synthesized
Trained	Troubleshot	Unified
Upgraded	Validated	Worked

Step Three: Select the best format to use.

Once you have decided which skills and experiences to highlight and which can be omitted, then you must select a resume format. We will discuss these formats in depth:

- Chronological resume

- Combination resume

- Contract resume

- Curriculum vitae (CV)

- Federal resumes

Chronological Resume

The tried-and-true chronological resume is the format most employers prefer to see. It's a simple format that lays out your qualifications in a timeline fashion, beginning with your most recent experience and working backward. It is best used if you have a proven track record in a specific career field and wish to remain in that field. In such a case, your resume is likely to illustrate career progression, and that is certainly a plus. This format also works with recent high school or college graduates.

As you can see, the chronological resume format clearly illustrates the candidate's contact information, general background, specific experience, and education.

John D. Smith

55 Sunset Drive ▪ Anyplace, Anystate 55555-5555 ▪ (555) 555-5555 ▪ jdsmith@email.com

PROFESSIONAL BACKGROUND SUMMARY

More than 21 years of technical and senior managerial telecommunications experience within the defense industry communications system. Proven ability to successfully organize and manage interoperability activities with combined forces worldwide. Able to effectively manage and coordinate tactical and fixed communications on domestic and international levels. Trained and experienced in staff operations and planning processes. Maintain current knowledge of emerging technologies. Bilingual in German/English. Possess a Department of Defense secret security clearance. Excellent leadership, communication, decision-making, technical, and organizational skills. Computer literate. Proficient using MS Windows applications. Received recognition on numerous occasions for superior and extraordinary work performance.

WORK EXPERIENCE

Chief, Transmissions Network Services Branch
Defense Information Systems Agency, Europe, 2004–Present

Manage a Department of Defense Agency program consisting of 40 personnel in support of a $100M annual effort to provide transmission services throughout Europe and the Balkans. Responsible for all aspects of Program Management of the European Transmissions Network Services. Conduct business case analysis and develop business plans for implementation. Identify customer needs and develop technical solutions to satisfy those requirements. Establish source of equipment and funding. Manage engineering, implementation, life-cycle support, and network management. Developed and implemented a plan supporting war fighter communications requirements in the Defense of Israel and Operation Iraqi Freedom, which integrated a diverse medium of terrestrial leases and military and commercial satellite bandwidths onto a common transmission platform spanning Southwest Asia, Europe, and the Continental U.S. Served as the management and operational lead for the installation of Defense Information Security Agency (DISA) presence points in Turkey and the Balkans.

Transmissions Network Engineer
Defense Information Systems Agency, Europe, 2001–2004

Served as lead engineer and manager for the installation of two new Global Information Grid (GIG) points of reference in Pristina and Camp Bondsteel, Kosovo. Effectively led efforts to identify user requirements, secure year-end funding, conduct site surveys, and perform final installation of these multimillion-dollar projects in less than 45 days, as opposed to the normal time of 6–12 months. Reduced call blocking on Camp Bondsteel by 400% and doubled the redundancy trunking out of Kosovo. Provided video backhaul services for three unmanned aerial vehicles during Enduring Freedom and IDNX/Promina configuration support for tactical satellite missions entering Tactical Entry Points in Europe. Supervised $18M Bosnia Command and Control Augmentation Program and transitioned downrange portions of the Joint Broadcast System (JBS) to the Global Broadcast System (GBS) without service interruption. Saved $200K per year by designing and installing a 10-node testbed and classroom facility.

Sample chronological resume.

(continued)

(continued)

John D. Smith   **Page Two**

Operations Manager
414ᵗʰ Signal Company, Mannheim, Germany, 2000–2001

Managed 230 employees while providing tactical communications support to Supreme Allied Commander Europe, Combined Joint Task Force, and subordinated headquarters within the North Atlantic Treaty Organization (NATO) framework. Planned, engineered, and implemented organizational missions. Efficiently conducted preplanning missions, contingency operations, and strategic readiness exercises on behalf of NATO organizations. Developed plan for the augmentation or replacement of the NATO Kosovo Force strategic network with tactical assets. Planned and implemented organization's deactivation. Disposed of $35M in unit property with no loss or damage. Organized and implemented an extensive occupational training exercise for all employees.

Manager
447ᵗʰ Signal Battalion, 15ᵗʰ Signal Brigade, Ft. Gordon, GA, 1997–2000

Managed 350 personnel in a communications training company. Planned, implemented, and evaluated programs providing joint service technicians with multichannel satellite operations and maintenance expertise. Maintained accurate accountability of a $20K budget and $300K worth of equipment. Ensured the billeting, safety, morale, and welfare of students. Coordinated with outside agencies to recommend and establish communications doctrine for a multiservice environment. Promoted positive community-wide relationships.

Assistant Manager
86ᵗʰ Signal Battalion, 269ᵗʰ Signal Company, Ft. Huachuca, AZ, 1995–1996

Ensured the organizational readiness of a tactical power-projection quick-reaction signal company, which provided command and control communications for deployed Army Forces headquarters and liaison teams worldwide. Directly supervised and counseled 40 technicians and ensured training for more than 160 employees. Accurately maintained accountability of property and equipment valued in excess of $38M. Authored operations plans and after-action reports. Managed a technical database.

EDUCATION AND TRAINING

- Bachelor of Arts degree, History, University of South Carolina, Aiken, SC, 1997
- Senior Management Course, Command and General Staff College, U.S. Army, 2000
- Advanced Signal Manager's Course, U.S. Army, 1996
- Branch Qualification Signal Officer's Course, U.S. Army, 1993
- Basic Field Manager's Training Course, U.S. Army, 1993
- Officer Candidate School, U.S. Army, 1992

Combination Resume

Sometimes the comfortable chronological format just doesn't cut it, however. Suppose you don't want to stay on your present career path. You want to do something different. Or perhaps you want to stay in your field, but you want to highlight specific skills and talents that may be buried in the timeline of a chronological format.

Enter the combination resume format for your marketing pleasure. The combination resume combines the chronological resume with what is known as a functional resume. Let's discuss the difference between the two for clarity's sake.

A functional resume is one that primarily highlights your skill areas and education versus your chronological work history. It usually does not reflect your work history, which is a critical factor to potential employers. (A purely functional resume would be more appropriate for a high school or college graduate who hasn't had any work experience at all.)

The combination resume, on the other hand, combines the strengths of both formats. It not only highlights your skills, abilities, and training, but it also provides the employer with the all-important work history of the chronological format. It is a highly adaptable resume that can be used in a number of situations and is therefore discussed here in lieu of the purely functional format.

On the following page is an example of the chronological resume used above, organized in a combination format.

As you can see in this example, the combination format nicely groups areas of expertise into summarizing paragraphs. It allows the employer to get a total feel for the applicant's depth of experience in one area versus trying to piece together all instances of experience throughout a given time period.

John D. Smith

55 Sunset Drive ▪ Anyplace, Anystate 55555-5555 ▪ (555) 555-5555 ▪ jdsmith@email.com

PROFESSIONAL BACKGROUND SUMMARY

More than 21 years of technical and senior managerial telecommunications experience within the defense industry communications system. Proven ability to successfully organize and manage interoperability activities with combined forces worldwide. Able to effectively manage and coordinate tactical and fixed communications on domestic and international levels. Trained and experienced in staff operations and planning processes. Maintain current knowledge of emerging technologies. Bilingual in German/English. Possess a Department of Defense secret security clearance. Excellent leadership, communication, decision-making, technical, and organizational skills. Computer literate. Proficient using MS Windows applications. Received recognition on numerous occasions for superior and extraordinary work performance.

WORK EXPERIENCE

Transmissions Network Management

Manage a Department of Defense Agency program consisting of 40 personnel in support of a $100M annual effort to provide transmissions services throughout Europe and the Balkans. Responsible for all aspects of Program Management of the European Transmissions Network Services. Conduct business case analysis and develop business plans for implementation. Identify customer needs and develop technical solutions to satisfy those requirements. Establish source of equipment and funding. Manage engineering, implementation, life-cycle support, and network management. Developed and implemented a plan supporting war fighter communications requirements in the Defense of Israel and Operation Iraqi Freedom, which integrated a diverse medium of terrestrial leases and military and commercial satellite bandwidths onto a common transmissions platform spanning Southwest Asia, Europe, and the Continental U.S. Served as the management and operational lead for the installation of Defense Information Security Agency (DISA) presence points in Turkey and the Balkans.

Network Engineering

Served as lead engineer and manager for the installation of two new Global Information Grid (GIG) points of reference in Pristina and Camp Bondsteel, Kosovo. Effectively led efforts to identify user requirements, secure year-end funding, conduct site surveys, and perform final installation of these multimillion-dollar projects in less than 45 days, as opposed to the normal time of 6–12 months. Reduced call blocking on Camp Bondsteel by 400% and doubled the redundancy trunking out of Kosovo. Provided video backhaul services for three unmanned aerial vehicles during Enduring Freedom and IDNX/Promina configuration support for tactical satellite missions entering Tactical Entry Points in Europe. Supervised $18M Bosnia Command and Control Augmentation Program and transitioned downrange portions of the Joint Broadcast System (JBS) to the Global Broadcast System (GBS) without service interruption. Saved $200K per year by designing and installing a 10-node testbed and classroom facility.

Sample combination resume.

John D. Smith   Page Two

Operations Management

Managed 230 employees while providing tactical communications support to Supreme Allied Commander Europe, Combined Joint Task Force, and subordinated headquarters within the North Atlantic Treaty Organization (NATO) framework. Planned, engineered, and implemented organizational missions. Efficiently conducted preplanning missions, contingency operations, and strategic readiness exercises on behalf of NATO organizations. Developed plan for the augmentation or replacement of the NATO Kosovo Force strategic network with tactical assets. Planned and implemented organization's deactivation. Disposed of $35M in unit property with no loss or damage. Organized and implemented an extensive occupational training exercise for all employees. Ensured the organizational readiness of a tactical power-projection quick-reaction signal company, which provided command and control communications for deployed Army Forces headquarters and liaison teams worldwide.

Training Management

Managed 350 personnel in a communications training company. Planned, implemented, and evaluated programs providing joint service technicians with multichannel satellite operations and maintenance expertise. Maintained accurate accountability of a $20K budget and $300K worth of equipment. Ensured the billeting, safety, morale, and welfare of students. Coordinated with outside agencies to recommend and establish communications doctrine for a multiservice environment. Promoted positive community-wide relationships.

WORK HISTORY

- **Chief, Transmissions Network Services Branch**
  Defense Information Systems Agency, Europe, 2004–Present

- **Transmissions Network Engineer**
  Defense Information Systems Agency, Europe, 2001–2004

- **Operations Manager**
  414th Signal Company, Mannheim, Germany, 2000–2001

- **Manager**
  447th Signal Battalion, 15th Signal Brigade, Ft. Gordon, GA, 1997–2000

- **Assistant Manager**
  86th Signal Battalion, 269th Signal Company, Ft. Huachuca, AZ, 1995–1996

EDUCATION AND TRAINING

- Bachelor of Arts degree, History, University of South Carolina, Aiken, SC, 1997
- Senior Management Course, Command and General Staff College, U.S. Army, 2000
- Advanced Signal Manager's Course, U.S. Army, 1996
- Branch Qualification Signal Officer's Course, U.S. Army, 1993
- Basic Field Manager's Training Course, U.S. Army, 1993
- Officer Candidate School, U.S. Army, 1992

Example Combination Skill Headings

In the process of developing a combination resume, you will need to clearly label your areas of expertise. If you are targeting a specific career field, this should be an easy task. Don't neglect, however, other areas that may support your job objective. The following lists provide you with ideas for identifying your areas of expertise:

Area: Management, Supervision, and Administration

- Management
- Quality Assurance
- Staff Development
- Problem Solving
- Program Analysis
- Supervision
- Logistics
- Program Management
- Professional Support
- Administration
- Coordination
- Conflict Resolution
- Statistical Analysis

Area: Communications, Information Management

- Communications
- Systems Analysis
- Satellite Control
- Technical Support
- Information Management
- Telecommunications
- Network Engineering
- Computer Security
- Equipment Maintenance
- Customer Service

Area: Office Administration

- Office Administration
- Accounts Management
- Office Automation
- Data Entry
- Correspondence
- Customer Relations
- Scheduling

Area: Sales and Training

- Market Research
- Advertising
- Testing
- Product Knowledge
- Customer Relations
- Program Development
- Training
- Market Analysis
- Purchasing
- Curriculum Evaluation
- Sales Management

Area: Technical, Mechanical, and Construction

- Schematics
- Projects
- Calibration
- Assembly
- Installation and Maintenance
- Technical Knowledge
- Diagnostics
- Transportation

Area: Transportation/Logistics

- Driving
- Transportation
- Safety
- Property Accountability
- Customer Service
- Instruction
- Hazardous Materials
- Shipping and Receiving
- Quality Control
- Vehicle Operations
- Environmental Safety
- Supply Management
- Inventory Management

Area: Food Service

- Menu Planning
- Food Storage
- Customer Service
- Nutrition
- Food Preparation
- Catering
- Facility Management

Contract Resume

Contract resumes defy all commonly accepted laws of resume writing. Accept that up front. A contract resume can run up to 20 pages, easily. It has a different purpose than your ordinary, run-of-the-mill resume.

Many prior military service members choose to work as civilians in the defense industry. The way a contract resume usually works is that you create your "ordinary" resume and submit it to a contractor. If your qualifications are well received along the way, you will probably be asked to revise your resume in a much more detailed fashion. This revision generally turns out to be a total rewrite of your resume in far more excruciating detail than you ever imagined.

If you want to work for this contractor, you must abide by their wishes. Their intent is not to torment you. They must show management, in explicit detail, how your qualifications match the exact requirements for a position working on a particular contract. (Note: If you are well known already to the contractor, they will probably forgo this step and ask you for the contract version right away.)

As you can see, the contract resume is the mother of all resumes. It ignores conventional resume wisdom, and that is acceptable in such a situation. Remember, the right resume format to use is the one that the employer wants to see in the first place.

JOHN D. SMITH

55 Sunset Drive ▪ Anyplace, Anystate 55555-5555 ▪ (555) 555-5555 ▪ jdsmith@email.com

SUMMARY OF EXPERTISE:

Network Engineering	Project Management
Testing and Certification	Network Management
Encryption Devices	Promina
Systems Engineering	Fiber Optics
Systems Life Cycle Development	Encoding/Decoding
Team Management	Integrated Digital Network Exchange
Site Engineering	Switch Multiplexing Units
Asynchronous Transfer Mode	Physical Plant Installation/Design
Satellite Earth Terminals	

WORK EXPERIENCE:

Chief, Transmissions Network Services Branch
April 2004–Present, U.S. Army, DISA Europe, Stuttgart, Germany
Duties/Responsibilities:
Responsible for all aspects of Program Management of the European Transmissions Network Services. Conduct business case analysis and develop business plans for implementation. Identify customer needs and develop technical solutions to satisfy those requirements. Establish source of equipment and funding. Manage engineering, implementation, life-cycle support, and network management. Developed and implemented a plan supporting war fighter communications requirements in the Defense of Israel and Operation Iraqi Freedom, which integrated a diverse medium of terrestrial leases and military and commercial satellite bandwidths onto a common transmission platform spanning Southwest Asia, Europe, and the Continental U.S. Served as the management and operational lead for the installation of Defense Information Security Agency (DISA) presence points in Turkey and the Balkans.

Network Engineer
May 2001–April 2004, U.S. Army, DISA Europe, Stuttgart, Germany
Duties/Responsibilities:
Responsible for network management and operations of a $100M communications network supporting the Defense Information Systems Network (DISN). Performed network trend and analysis to identify potential network congestion and problem areas and then engineered solutions to mitigate those potential network problems. Identified customer requirements and engineered solutions to fulfill those requirements. Served as lead engineer and manager for the installation of two new Global Information Grid (GIG) points of presence in Pristina and Camp Bondsteel, Kosovo. Led efforts to identify user requirements, secure year-end funding, conduct site surveys, and perform final installation of these multimillion-dollar projects in less than 45 days, as opposed to the normal time of 6–12 months. Reduced call blocking on Camp Bondsteel by 400% and doubled the redundancy trunking out of Kosovo. Provided video backhaul services for unmanned aerial vehicles during Enduring Freedom and IDNX/Promina configuration support for tactical satellite missions entering Standard Tactical Entry Points (STEP) in Europe. Supervised $18M Bosnia Command and Control Augmentation Program and transitioned Balkans portions of the Joint Broadcast System (JBS) to the Global Broadcast System (GBS) without service interruption. Saved $200K per year by designing and installing a 10-node test bed and classroom facility.

Sample contract resume.

(continued)

(continued)

JOHN D. SMITH, Page Two

Operations Officer/Executive Officer
November 2000–May 2001, 414th Signal Company, Allied Forces North, NATO, Mannheim, Germany
Duties/Responsibilities:
Engineered, installed, and operated a tactical communications network to support Supreme Allied Commander Europe, Combined Joint Task Force, and subordinated headquarters within the North Atlantic Treaty Organization (NATO) framework. Planned, engineered, and implemented organizational missions. Developed plan for the augmentation or replacement of the NATO Kosovo Force strategic network with tactical assets. Planned and implemented organization's deactivation. Disposed of $35M in unit property with no loss or damage. Organized and implemented an extensive occupational training exercise for all employees.

Company Commander
April 1998–November 2000, Company B, 447th Signal Battalion, Fort Gordon, Georgia
Duties/Responsibilities:
Trained Department of Defense personnel on the engineering, installation, operations, and maintenance of satellite earth terminal equipment, including AN/TSC–100, AN/TSC-85, AN/TSC-94, AN/TSC-93, and AN/GSC-52. Also provided training on the operations and control of the Defense Satellite Communications Systems. Planned, implemented, and evaluated programs of instruction, providing joint service technicians with multichannel satellite operations and maintenance expertise. Coordinated with outside agencies to recommend and establish communications doctrine for a multiservice environment. Managed 350 personnel.

Assistant Brigade Operations Officer
January 1997–April 1998, 15th Signal Brigade, Fort Gordon, Georgia
Duties/Responsibilities:
Responsible for the development and evaluation of training Department of Defense personnel on strategic and tactical communications systems. Training included all wire, radio, multiplexing, and switching.

Executive Officer
May 1995–December 1996, 269th Signal Company, Fort Huachuca, Arizona
Duties/Responsibilities:
Installed, operated, and maintained the AN/TSC-85, AN-TSC-93, and AN/TSC-143 satellite earth terminals; AN/TRC-173 and AN/TRC-174 Line of Sight (LOS) microwave terminals; AN/TTC 39D circuit and packet switch; Mobile Gateway Internet Interface Van; Switch Multiplexing Units; AN/PSC-3 and MST-20 single-channel satellite radios; and all high-frequency radios. Performed frequency management engineering for multiple- and single-channel satellite and radio transmissions.

JOHN D. SMITH, Page Three

Assistant Battalion Operations Officer/Force Modernization Officer
January 1995–May 1995, 86th Signal Battalion, Fort Huachuca, Arizona
Duties/Responsibilities:
Force Modernization Officer for an Echelon Above Corps Signal Battalion. Coordinated with industry to develop technical solutions and platforms that upgraded or replaced current capabilities. Provided installation and testing support for fielding numerous communications and support systems, including AN/TTC-39D circuit and packet switch, AN/TSC-143 Triband satellite and switching earth terminal, Mobile Gateway Internet Interface Van, and Tactical Quiet Generators. Planned and conducted network interoperability exercises to test the interface between new systems and currently fielded communications equipment. Conducted evaluations of communications equipment worldwide with the cooperation of the Joint Interoperability Test Center. Evaluated all hardware, software, and training requirements for new equipment fieldings. Planned and coordinated the activation of the Army's first Power Projection for Army Command, Control, and Communications Signal Company.

Detachment Commander/Operations Officer
July 1994–January 1995, 385th Signal Company, Camp Doha, Kuwait
Duties/Responsibilities:
Commanded an Echelons Above Corps signal detachment consisting of multiple and single satellite systems supporting CENTCOM, NAVCENT, and ARCENT. Engineered, installed, operated, and maintained AN/TSC-85 multichannel satellite terminal and the Digital Communications Satellite Subsystems (DCSS). Maintained, repaired, and operated AN/PSC-3 single-channel satellite systems. Provided baseband user interface engineering support, including frequency spectrum management for satellite access frequencies, times, and bandwidth. Reengineered equipment to bypass the baseband portion of the AN/TSC-85 utilizing the DCSS equipment to increase communications systems interoperability and improve systems interface. Performed fault isolation of all network communications equipment down to the lowest replaceable unit. Installed, operated, and maintained AN/TSC-85 and AN/TSC-93 satellite earth terminals; AN/TRC-173, AN/TRC-174, and AN/TRC-138 Line of Sight (LOS) microwave terminals; AN/TTC-39D tactical telephone switch; and AN/TYC-39A tactical message switch. Responsible for all strategic and tactical communications for the U.S. Army in Kuwait. Performed communications systems interoperability engineering for American, British, and Kuwaiti services. Performed upgrades and troubleshooting of computer communications systems with fault isolation to the lowest replaceable unit.

Transmissions Platoon Leader
November 1993–July 1994, 505th Signal Company, Fort Huachuca, Arizona
Duties/Responsibilities:
Transmissions Platoon Leader in an Echelons Above Corps Signal Battalion. Planned, installed, operated, maintained, and managed communications networks in support of joint and combined operations worldwide. Engineered, installed, operated, and maintained AN/TSC-85 and AN/TSC-93 satellite earth terminals, AN/TRC-138 SHF LOS terminals, AN/TRC-170 tropospheric scatter terminals, AN/TTC-39D tactical telephone switch, and AN/TYC-39A message switch. Performed frequency management functions for satellite and radio transmissions.

(continued)

(continued)

JOHN D. SMITH, Page Four

Operations Noncommissioned Officer
April 1989–May 1992, 52nd Signal Battalion, Stuttgart, Germany
Duties/Responsibilities:
Planned and managed strategic communications network in support of Headquarters, European Command, and NATO. Provided technical support to ensure maximum reliability of radio and wire critical command and control communications networks. Installed, operated, and maintained communications systems supporting the World Wide Multi-Media Exchange Communications System, the Automated Multi-Media Exchange, the Computer Support Processor, the Telecommunications Center, and the Special Security Office. Responsible for the test, evaluation, and acceptance of secure communications systems.

Automatic Secure Voice Technician
October 1987–March 1989, 578th Signal Company, Stuttgart, Germany
Duties/Responsibilities:
Installed, operated, and maintained the AN/FTC-31 secure voice switch and Secure Voice Access Console. Operated and maintained STU-II and STU-III secure voice terminals; Narrow Band Subscriber Terminals; and wideband subscriber terminals, including KY-3, HY-2, KG-30 family, KG-80 family, KW-26, KG-13, and KW-7 secure communications equipment. Installed, operated, and maintained secure data communications equipment. Responsible for the maintenance and repair of data and voice traffic terminating equipment and associated transmissions path. Responsible for the test, evaluation, and acceptance of the first Defense Red Switch in Europe.

Switch Technician
August 1986–May 1987, Claydesta Communications, Dallas, Texas
Duties/Responsibilities:
Installed, operated, and maintained Harris 20/20 and Nortel 3000 telephone switches. Engineering and network management of a regional long-distance communications network to include all internal wiring and cabling to support customer service and tandem switch trunks. Performed fault isolation of the system to the lowest replaceable unit.

Automatic Secure Voice Technician
June 1983–June 1986, 578th Signal Company, Stuttgart, Germany
Duties/Responsibilities:
Installed, operated, and maintained the AN/FTC-31 secure voice switch and Secure Voice Access Console. Operated and maintained STU-II and STU-III secure voice terminals; Narrow Band Subscriber Terminals; and wideband subscriber terminals, including KY-3, HY-2, KG-30 family, KG-80 family, KW-26, KG-13, and KW-7 secure communications equipment. Installed, operated, and maintained secure data communications equipment. Maintained and repaired data and voice traffic terminating equipment and associated transmissions paths.

CERTIFICATIONS & TRAINING SUMMARY
Promina Certification, 2002

TECHNICAL TRAINING:
Secure Telephone Unit Maintenance Course, Bad Tolz, Germany, 1984
Secure Voice Switch Course, Fort Gordon, Georgia, 1983
Fixed Ciphony Repairer's Course, Fort Gordon, Georgia, 1982

JOHN D. SMITH, Page Five

RELEVANT TRAINING:
North Atlantic Treaty Organization Staff Officer Course, Oberammergau, Germany, 2000
Combined Arms Services Staff School, Command and General Staff College, Fort Leavenworth, Kansas, 2000
Equal Opportunity Senior Leaders Course, Fort Gordon, Georgia, 1998
Cadre Training Course, Fort Gordon, Georgia, 1998
Signal Officers Advanced Course, Fort Gordon, Georgia, 1996
Junior Maintenance Officer Course, Fort Knox, Kentucky, 1994
Signal Officer's Branch Qualification Course, Fort Gordon, Georgia, 1993
Infantry Officer's Basic Course, Fort Benning, Georgia, 1993
Officer Candidate School, Fort Benning, Georgia, 1992
Military Forms and Report Writing, Stuttgart, Germany, 1989
Effective Military Writing, Stuttgart, Germany, 1989
Primary Leadership Development Course, Augsburg, Germany, 1989

SIGNIFICANT CAREER ACCOMPLISHMENTS/AWARDS:
1992 Distinguished Military Graduate, Officer Candidate School, Fort Benning, GA, 1992
1989 Commandants List, Primary Leadership Development Course, Augsburg, Germany, 1989

PROFESSIONAL AFFILIATIONS:
AUSA—Member

SECURITY CLEARANCE: Secret

Curriculum Vitae (CV)

In some instances, you may find that you need a formal document that highlights more than just your work history or skills and abilities. You may need to list such detail as your publications, presentations, honors, and professional affiliations. This is where the curriculum vitae, also known simply as CV, comes into play. It is used primarily by those seeking employment in such professions as education, research, medicine, or science. Formats for the CV may vary. The following outline represents one option:

HEADING

[Name, Address, Telephone, and E-mail.]

EDUCATION

[Degree(s) earned. List topic of dissertation if applicable. List any other specialized training in your field.]

PROFESSIONAL EXPERIENCE

[Record your work experience relative to the field here.]

PUBLICATIONS

[Subcategorize here using titles such as Books and Book Chapters Written, Book Reviews, Works in Progress.]

PRESENTATIONS

[Indicate whether you were an invited guest speaker. Include the topic of your presentation as well as the date and the name of the organization to which you made the presentation.]

RECOGNITIONS AND HONORS

[List any recognitions and honors you have received.]

PROFESSIONAL ORGANIZATIONS

[List memberships you have in professional societies and associations.]

OTHER PROFESSIONAL ACTIVITIES

[List your memberships on committees of professional societies and any offices you have within those organizations.]

OTHER INDICATORS OF SCHOLARSHIP

[List anything here that doesn't fit neatly in the above categories such as contracts received, reviews of your work, etc.]

Federal Resumes

If you are targeting a position in the federal government, you may find that traditional resume guidelines don't apply. In fact, what you will most likely find is that each position may have different application requirements. You may have the option to use what is known as a federal resume in lieu of a standard application form.

Federal resumes must include the following:

Job Information

- Announcement number, title, grade of the position you seek

Personal Information

- Your full name, mailing address, and day and evening telephone numbers
- Your citizenship

Veterans' Preference

Your service in the military may assist you in obtaining preference for employment with the federal government after your life in uniform. This assumes that you were separated under honorable conditions.

If your military service began after October 15, 1976, you must have a Campaign Badge, Expeditionary Medal, or a service-connected disability in order to claim Veterans' Preference for a federal job. If you are targeting a position in the Senior Executive

Service or a job where competition is limited to status candidates (those already in career or career-conditional employment status), Veterans' Preference is not a factor.

In order to claim a 5-point Veterans' Preference, attach a copy of your DD 214, Certificate of Release or Discharge from Active Duty, or other proof of eligibility to your application packet.

To claim a 10-point Veterans' Preference, attach an SF 15, Application for 10-Point Veterans' Preference, to your application, plus any other requested documentation.

Reinstatement Eligibility

- If you have previous federal employment experience (excluding uniformed military service), you must list the highest federal civilian grade held along with the job series and dates held.

Education

You may be required to submit official or unofficial copies of transcripts for some positions. In most cases, you will nonetheless be required to submit the names and address of educational institutions you have attended:

- High School (include the name, city, state, and ZIP code)

- Colleges and universities attended along with your major(s) and types and years of degree(s) earned

Work Experience

You will need to provide a history of your work experience to include the following:

- Job titles

- Duties and accomplishments

- Employer's name and address

- Supervisor's name and phone number

- Starting and ending dates of employment (month and year)

- Hours worked per week

- Salary earned on an annual, hourly, or monthly basis

You will also need to state on your federal resume whether or not your present employer may be contacted.

Other Qualifications

It would be to your advantage to include other qualifications not listed elsewhere on your resume. For example, list your job-related training courses completed or your job-related skills. Additionally, any licenses or certificates you have earned should be noted as well as any noteworthy honors received.

For more information regarding federal resumes, consult the *Federal Resume Guidebook* by Kathryn Kraemer Troutman for more details. You can also visit her Web site at www.resumeplace.com.

You may also be required to supplement your resume or job application with any number of additional forms, question-naires, or narratives addressing various knowledges, skills, and abilities, also known simply as KSAs. The level of detail that you supply regarding these KSAs can be related to the level of position you are seeking. Criteria differ depending upon the agency offering the job.

The application, interviewing, and selection process involved in federal employment is usually long and tedious. This is not always the case, but be prepared for that scenario.

Step Four: Identify additional experience and include as appropriate.

Again, there is some disagreement between resume experts regarding unusual experience. Just what is considered appropriate experience versus what isn't depends largely upon the job. For example, highlighting your superior weapons marksmanship would probably not be a good idea for a senior management level position within corporate America. If, however, you're applying for a position within law enforcement, it becomes relevant. In such a case, one could even argue that it is more of a job-related skill than an optional category.

In any event, be careful about the extras that you may be inclined to include on your resume. Generally speaking, the following types of information are *verboten:*

- Age
- Height
- Weight
- Salary requirements
- Salary history
- Political affiliation
- Religious beliefs
- Marital status
- Condition of physical health

The acid test here is this: Does including this information directly support your objective? If it does, include it. If it doesn't, leave it off. For example, an aspiring model would probably include his or her age, height, and weight. A personnel manager would not.

Step Five: Review, edit, and revise your resume as necessary.

After you've completed your first draft, put it away for a day or so. You can easily find yourself a victim of tunnel vision. When that happens, you are usually mortified later to realize you omitted something important from your resume. Just give it a break and go back to it in a day or so when you can look at it again with fresh, objective eyes.

You are never going to get to a point where your resume is completed. That may be discouraging to hear, but it's the truth. As you apply for different positions, even if they fall in the same career field, you should review, edit, and revise your resume as necessary to best target it for a given opportunity. It requires a bit more effort, but your resume will stand out from the others if you take those extra steps.

What to Do with Your Resume After You're Hired

The temptation may be great to file your resume away once you've been hired. That's not the best idea. Now that you've spent so much time and effort on it, keep it updated. You never know when you will need it again. Having it available and up-to-date at all times is not only prudent, it is a necessity in the ever-changing world of work.

Resume Writing Tips Worth Reviewing

You need not be a writing guru to develop an effective resume. You simply need to select the most appropriate format and keep in mind the following tips as you craft your document:

- Use power words that clearly identify your skills and experiences.

- Refrain from using personal pronouns such as "I," "me," or "my."

- Use a consistent tense in your sentence fragments throughout your resume.

- Avoid random capitalization.

- Use words that you know; don't try to sound like someone you're not.

- Don't rely solely on your computer's spell- and grammar-checking tools.

- Don't create endless sentences by using semicolons. You are not creating a military performance review or copying a job description. Use periods at the ends of your sentence fragments. It's okay to have varying lengths.

- Use appropriate and correct punctuation.

- Keep your resume to no more than two pages, unless directed otherwise by the employer.

- Use an attractive, easy-to-read sans serif font at 10, 11, or 12 points in size.

- Don't type your resume in all capital letters.

- Don't over-format your resume with bullets, underlines, and bold and/or italic letters, particularly if it is destined for scanning. Scanners don't always pick up the finer formats, and the reader could be left with a resume full of strange symbols rather than your intended formatting.

- If faxing your resume, use plain bond paper rather than heavier stationery.

- If using stationery, keep it conservative in color (white and cream are the best shades to use for easier reproduction purposes).

- If your stationery has a watermark on it (hold it up to the light to see if it does), insert it in the printer so that the watermark can be read from left to right once your resume has been printed.

- If mailing your resume, use a standard business-sized envelope rather than the oversized variety.

- If you are creating a cover letter to go with your resume, use matching stationery and headings.

- Keep a one-inch margin around your resume. The empty space actually makes your resume appear more attractive and organized than if you attempted to use every inch of space.

- If you are e-mailing your resume to someone, ensure that it gets there not only by attaching the file to the message but also by cutting and pasting it from your word processor onto your e-mail message, just below your "cover letter."

CHAPTER 6 Creating Effective Job Search Letters

One of the key components to any successful job search lies in the effectiveness of your communication skills. You have to be able to tell someone all about your skills, abilities, and experiences as they relate to the position available. You do this in a couple ways. You write your resume and make sure it gets to the right person. If you're lucky, you interview for a job either face-to-face or via the telephone.

Before you get that opportunity, however, you usually find yourself writing a cover letter to send along with your resume. Maybe you find yourself trying to compose a thank-you letter after an interview or after someone has helped you in some significant way. Perhaps you receive the dreaded "Thanks, but no thanks" letter and choose to respond to it. There are many occasions where you will find yourself in need of effective written communication skills.

A cover letter is simply a letter of introduction that usually accompanies your resume. It should not exceed one page and it should clearly and effectively convince the employer to give your resume the time of day. If you are e-mailing your resume, the e-mail message itself is your cover letter.

You may spend a great deal of time creating, editing, and revising your resume. Don't jeopardize your chances by breezing through the cover letter without any real thought.

Will employers actually read your cover letter? Yes, they will and no, they won't. It depends on who is processing the mail and how he or she chooses to deal with it. Job opportunities have been lost and won depending on the effectiveness of the basic cover letter.

The Parts of a Cover Letter

Let's take a quick look at the basic parts of the cover letter. Warning—this is not exciting stuff, but neither should it be ignored. It's important that you take the time to create a great cover letter as it could determine whether or not actual interviews come your way. That makes it a little more exciting, don't you think?

The parts we will examine here include the following:

- The heading
- The dateline
- The addressee
- The salutation
- The introduction
- The main body
- The conclusion
- The signature block

The Heading

If you look at the heading on your resume, you'll see your name and your contact information. This is how the heading on your cover letter should also appear. In fact, it should match the information and layout of the heading on your resume exactly. Remember, this section should not go into overkill on contact numbers and it should clearly show the employer how to easily contact you.

The Dateline

After your heading, you should skip a couple of lines and insert the date. Avoid using abbreviations and military-style formatting in this section and throughout your cover letter. For example, don't use *2 Jan 06* or *2/6/06*. Instead use, *January 2, 2006*. Be sure you don't revert to such abbreviations or military formatting later in the letter, either. Old habits die hard.

The Addressee

Who is the recipient of your letter? Do you know? If not, you need to go back to square one and do a little investigative work.

Always send your cover letter and resume to an actual person rather than a department title if at all possible. Doing so will illustrate your level of genuine interest in the position. Anyone can address a letter to the Human Resources Director. The candidate that takes the initiative to pick up the telephone and find out to whom the letter should be addressed stands out from others who didn't. Use the telephone to find out correct names and addresses. Never misspell words in any of your job search letters or on your resume. The spell check on your word processing software will be helpful, but remember that some spellings are unique and won't appear in the dictionary. Take the time to get them right or you might find that you're not considered a serious candidate.

The Salutation

This section seems like it would be easy enough, but there are a couple of common pitfalls. Believe it or not, your salutation can actually set the tone for your cover letter. If you write *Dear Sir or Madam* or *To Whom It May Concern*, it will suggest that you have not made the effort to find out to whom you are writing. If you write *Dear Susan* rather than *Dear Mrs. Jones*, it will suggest a familiarity with the reader. Be sure it is a genuine one rather than a hopeful one. If you write *Dear Mr. Terry McDonald* when the recipient is in fact *Ms. Terrie McDonald*, that will speak volumes as well. Never forget that small details to you are not so small to others.

The Introduction

As mentioned above, the cover letter shouldn't be more than one page. The introduction will probably take up one paragraph of your total page. In this section, you will briefly introduce your intentions, avoiding the "My name is so-and-so" approach at all costs. (Your heading took care of telling the reader your name.) In the introduction, you tell the employer specifically why you are writing the letter. Tell him what position you are interested in and how you learned about it. Be specific. If someone recommended that you write this person, mention that name only if the relationship between the person making the recommendation and the reader is a good one.

The Main Body

In the next paragraph or two, you want to show the employer how your skills match what he or she is in the market to buy. You should know what specific attributes the employer is seeking at this point. If you have them, tell him in this section. If available to you, use the same words that the employer used to advertise the position, assuming you do have those same skills. Don't make the mistake of repeating your resume in the main body; however, you must communicate your skills concisely and interestingly enough so that the person holding your cover letter will want to take a look at your resume.

The Conclusion

Make your call to action in the conclusion of your cover letter. This means that you not only thank the reader for his or her consideration, but you try to determine the next step. Here is an example:

> Thank you for your consideration of my qualifications. I will call you the week of September 15 to answer any questions you may have regarding my resume. If you would like

Jill D. Smith

12345 South Any Street ▪ Anywhere, TX 55555 ▪ (555) 555-5555 ▪ jilldsmith@email.com

January 15, 2005

David Smith
Media Services International
Human Resources Department
2626 Dulles Way
Seattle, WA 55555

Dear Mr. Smith:

Enclosed is my resume for your review. I am interested in applying for the Public Affairs Specialist position that was advertised in last Sunday's *Seattle Times News*. The attached resume provides details concerning my qualifications and background.

As you can see, I have worked extensively in Air Force public affairs for the past seven years. Specifically, I served as editor for various sections of a newspaper distributed throughout the European Theater of operations. I coordinated news coverage with all branches of the military and managed the information flow for senior executive personnel. I am comfortable working in a fast-paced, unpredictable environment. Additionally, I hold a current Department of Defense security clearance.

Having reached my goals in the military, I now eagerly anticipate returning to the Greater Seattle area, where I hope to meet new challenges within your organization. I will contact you the week of February 1 to answer any questions you may have regarding my resume. If you would like to contact me before then, please do so.

Sincerely,

Jill D. Smith

Sample cover letter.

to contact me before then, I can be reached at the above telephone number or e-mail address.

The Signature Block

The signature block should contain your final sign-off, your typed name and your signature placed in between the two sections. (An example cover letter appears on page 129.) Examples of appropriate sign-offs include *Respectfully, Sincerely, Regards, or With Warm Regards.*

As you can see, the cover letter on page 129 is clearly and concisely written. It is addressed to a person versus a title, which promotes the likelihood of it actually being read. It tells the employer immediately why he is holding the letter in his hands and it briefly highlights the candidate's applicable experience. In her closing, note that she proactively takes the next step into her own hands. This is an excellent cover letter example.

Thank-You Letters

Quick, who should you send a thank-you letter to and when should you do it? The answer might surprise you. Of course, you should always send one to an employer after an interview. If you interviewed with more than one person, send a letter of thanks to each one. It's not brown-nosing raised to a new level. It's common courtesy and could make the difference in whether or not you get the job. You should also send a thank-you letter to anyone who has helped you in your job search process, whether you have interviewed with them or not. Again, this is a common courtesy that could reap uncommon benefits.

If it is typewritten, the thank-you letter should contain the following:

- A heading
- The date
- The addressee
- The salutation

- The main body

- The conclusion

- The signature block

The biggest difference between the cover letter and the thank-you letter can be found in the main body and the conclusion. The main body of the thank-you letter should be about one to two paragraphs in length. It should thank the employer for his time. Remind him of when you interviewed and the position you discussed. Use this section as a tool to give the employer your initial impressions of the job and take the opportunity to remind the employer why you are the right person for the position. If there was something said at the interview that seemed to impress your potential future boss, remind him of it here. Or if you neglected to mention something important that could change the way he views your candidacy, certainly add that information here.

In the conclusion, go for broke. If you want the job, say so. Ask the employer to give you the job. Why not? Even if you're not sure you want the job, be confident in this letter that you do. Your goal in an effective job search is to generate choices. You have to have them to make them.

You may decide to take a more personal approach in creating your thank-you letter by handwriting it. If you do this, use professional looking stationery or a notecard. Write neatly as a hastily written, hard-to-read note will only suggest that your work would reflect the same standard. (There is something to be said for handwriting analysis!) Your thank-you note should include the date, the salutation, a brief paragraph thanking the employer for his time and consideration, a mention of your continued interest in the position, an appropriate sign-off, and your signature.

The thank-you letter is a small yet powerful tool. As you can see, it needn't be a complicated undertaking. It just needs to have a positive effect. Details count.

Jill D. Smith
12345 South Any Street ▪ Anywhere, TX 55555 ▪ (555) 555-5555 ▪ jilldsmith@email.com

February 20, 2005

David Smith
Media Services International
Human Resources Department
2626 Dulles Way
Seattle, WA 55555

Dear Mr. Smith:

Thank you for your time during our interview yesterday. I truly appreciated the information you were able to provide me regarding the Public Affairs Specialist position.

After learning more about this position during our interview, I am convinced that this is the job for me. I know that my background, coupled with my enthusiasm and willingness to travel, would prove to be a real asset to your organization.

Again, thank you. I look forward to hearing from you in the near future.

Sincerely,

Jill D. Smith

Sample thank-you letter.

Networking Letters

A networking letter is simply a letter you write to someone who might be able to help you in your job search. It may be a letter to someone you already know or not. It may include a copy of your resume or not. If it doesn't include a copy of your resume, it should include a detailed, yet concise, description of your skills, abilities, and work experience. You may send it to someone who has a job opening or to someone who can help you get into contact with someone who does.

Like all job search letters, the networking letter should be kept to a minimum length, with one page being best. Use the networking letter as a flexible tool in your search. Don't rely on it solely. The best approach in networking is to talk with someone either face to face or on the telephone. A networking letter could be used as a follow-up hybrid thank-you/networking letter after such a conversation. It should include the basic components of any letter:

- A heading
- The date
- The addressee
- The salutation
- The main body
- The conclusion
- The signature block

Networking letters, as well as phone calls, can be a real boost to your efforts. As a safeguard, always be sure you have the blessing of the person whose name you're dropping before you do so.

Jill D. Smith
12345 South Any Street ▪ Anywhere, TX 55555 ▪ (555) 555-5555 ▪ jilldsmith@email.com

February 10, 2005

Samantha Roselie
Media Services International
News Desk
2626 Dulles Way
Seattle, WA 55555

Dear Ms. Roselie,

Mr. Jason D. Smith, a mutual acquaintance of ours, suggested that I contact you regarding potential employment with your organization. He mentioned that you may be in the market for a new Public Affairs Specialist in the near future.

I am currently in the process of leaving the U.S. Air Force after seven years of honorable service, working specifically within the public affairs arena. I have enjoyed my tenure in the military and have accumulated many valuable experiences and skills. I am interested in staying in my current field, perhaps as a member of your staff.

I have taken the liberty of enclosing my resume for your review. If you feel there may be a possibility for a career fit, I would welcome further discussion. Thank you in advance for your kind consideration.

Sincerely,

Jill D. Smith

Sample networking letter.

The Letter Resume

There is a fine line between the networking letter and the letter resume. In essence, the letter resume is a detailed cover letter that doesn't include a copy of your resume. You can use it for networking purposes or for applying for a job. The more traditional approach is to simply use the cover letter and the resume as the case warrants. On occasion, however, you might find the letter resume a useful tool in your job search bag of tricks.

As you can read here, there is slightly more detail in the resume letter. It gets into a few more work-related details as opposed to the networking letter. Both types of letters can be used effectively in your campaign.

Get It in Writing

Let's suppose for a moment that you've verbally been offered a job. While most employers will follow up their offer in a written contract, some will not. It is rare that this happens, but it could. If this happens to you, take the time to construct a letter to the employer that clearly states the terms of your agreement and print it up twice. Include a signature block for yourself and for your employer. Provide instructions for him to sign both copies after reading it and return one copy to you. Don't be concerned that this creates an atmosphere of distrust. Indeed, it creates the opposite. By clearly stating the conditions of your employment with the company, you avoid any future misunderstandings and disappointments. Again, it is rare that you will be offered a position that isn't put clearly in writing.

The Mechanics of Letter Construction

Dress your letters for success just as you would dress yourself for an interview. Your job search letters will stand an increased chance of actually being read by others if you take the time to construct them in a professional manner.

Jill D. Smith
12345 South Any Street ▪ Anywhere, TX 55555 ▪ (555) 555-5555 ▪ jilldsmith@email.com

February 10, 2005

Samantha Roselie
Media Services International
News Desk
2626 Dulles Way
Seattle, WA 55555

Dear Ms. Roselie,

Mr. Jason D. Smith, a mutual acquaintance of ours, suggested that I contact you regarding potential employment with your organization. He mentioned that you may be in the market for a new Public Affairs Specialist in the near future.

I am currently in the process of leaving the U.S. Air Force after seven years of honorable service, working specifically within the public affairs arena. I have enjoyed my tenure in the military and have accumulated many valuable experiences and skills. I am interested in staying in my current field, perhaps as a member of your staff.

My most recent experience has been within the European Theater of Operations, specifically in the Kaiserslautern, Germany, American Military Community. During my three years as a public relations specialist, I have had the opportunity to work with senior-executive-level military and civilian community members and visiting dignitaries from European Union countries. Prior to that, I worked in the Air Force's Washington, D.C., Public Affairs Office for four years. My verbal and written communication skills are excellent. Additionally, my public speaking and reporting skills have been recognized by my supervisors as being superior. I would be more than happy to provide you with a list of my references, should you be interested.

If you feel there may be a possibility for a career fit, I would welcome further discussion. Thank you in advance for your kind consideration.

Sincerely,

Jill D. Smith

Sample letter resume.

Letter Size

All of your job search letters should be as brief, but as thorough, as possible. Try to limit them to no more than one page.

Typeface Recommendations and Enhancements

There are a variety of fonts available to you within a given word processor. Stick to the classic, professional looking fonts for the best appearance. The following are recommended:

- Times New Roman, 11 point

- Times New Roman, 12 point

- Arial, 11 point

- Arial, 12 point

- Arial Narrow, 12 point

If you are creating your document for an e-mail, you may be able to make the font even smaller once it is in your actual e-mail message. This will depend on your Internet service and the features available to you. If you are doing this, draft your letter in a word processing document first and then copy it into your e-mail message. This will prevent you from feeling rushed while writing it, or worse, from accidentally sending it before it's ready.

No matter what anyone says, size really does matter. The font size of your job search letters should be neither too small nor too large. Make it easy for the employer to read it.

Enhancements such as bolding, underlines, italics, and graphics should be kept to a minimum, particularly on job search letters. They can look nice if used sparingly and with a purpose in mind. For example, suppose the company logo your intended target uses includes double underlines. You might consider incorporating double underlines somewhere on your letter. This may subconsciously suggest to the reader that you could fit into their organization. It's not exactly a proven science, but it couldn't hurt either.

If your resume is being scanned into a database, however, you will want to eliminate such visuals altogether as their existence doesn't translate well. For example, bullets maybe actually be read as question marks. Maybe this will change later as technology evolves, but for now, stick to the basic text in these cases.

Paper Types

Just as there are a number of fonts available to use, there is a variety of paper out there as well. As for colors of paper, you can choose from chartreuse, slate blue, or banana yellow if the creative urge is there. It would be in your best interest, though, to stick with basic white or cream. Not to stifle your creativity, but basic white photocopies best, and hopefully that is what will happen to your credentials as they are passed around the firm.

If you are faxing your documents, use plain bond paper. Save the 20-20 pound watermarked stationery for other times when you are either mailing or hand-carrying your letters.

Formats

In the military, there are entire regulations that tell you specifically how to create correspondence. If you have this publication, burn it. You don't need it in your search for a civilian job whatsoever. You can be flexible in formatting your letters—just make sure they are consistent in format and present a professional appearance.

CHAPTER 7 Winning Interview Skills

If you're diligent, your job search efforts will ultimately result in an interview. This is your time to shine and to show a potential employer that you would be an incredible asset to his or her organization. It is also a time for you to fully investigate whether an opportunity is suited to your talents, skills, and taste. A job interview is truly a two-sided event, and if you keep that thought in mind, you'll minimize any interview jitters.

Understanding the Interview Process

You may have sat on military board reviews before, but civilian interviews have nothing in common with them. First of all, there are different *types* of interviews, each having a different purpose. The three basic types are as follows:

- The Informational interview
- The Screening interview
- The Employment interview

The Informational Interview

The informational interview is an excellent way to gather, you guessed it, information about a particular employer or career field. It is an equally excellent way to network yourself into a circle of influence that could prove far-reaching in your own career endeavors. Don't underestimate the value of such an interview. It could open doors for you like no other.

The Screening Interview

Time is money, and employers don't like to waste it either. The screening interview is a useful tool for everyone's mutual benefit. It allows both parties to determine whether any future association is plausible. It can happen in any number of formats, including telephone, e-mail, teleconferencing, or in person. It is often a conversation initiated by someone other than the decision maker, but not always.

The Employment Interview

This is the mother of all interviews. It is the one that leads (or not) to employment in an actual position within an organization. Employment interviews can be held in a formal or informal setting. They can be conducted by one or more individuals. You can participate in only one interview or in a whole series of them. In short, there is no single definition of what constitutes such an event. That's what makes the whole process so fun, don't you think?

Tips, Techniques, and Tricks of the Trade

Essentially, employers want to know three things about you, even if they don't come right out and say it. They want to know whether

- You can do the job
- You will do the job
- You will fit in with their organization

It's up to you to communicate your ability, willingness, and flexibility.

You can view the interview itself in one of two ways. It can be a stressful occasion for which you fail to prepare. Or you can take the better approach by understanding the interview process for what it truly is.

The interview process is just that—a process. It is an opportunity for you and the employer to meet and find common ground. You both want to make the right choices for your own interests. You can't possibly do that until you learn more about each other. View the interview as a learning experience. You will be questioned, yes. You will also have the chance to ask your own questions.

The key to making the process effective for you is simple research. You must know something about the company and about the position before you interview for it. It is assumed that you have already begun this process, as you applied for the job. Now, you need to dig a little deeper so that you look like a serious contender in the face-to-face meeting.

Again, because the point bears repeating, the whole idea of the interview process is to generate choices so that you can make an educated decision concerning your future career after gathering all the pertinent facts. The rest of this chapter breaks the interview down into the proverbial before, during, and after portions and looks at time-honored and proven strategies for success at each stage.

Before the Interview

Successful interviews usually don't occur all by themselves. They happen because the job seeker has taken the time to thoughtfully organize and prepare for the event. The following suggestions can help you to do just that.

Get your facts straight.

There is a certain element of excitement involved in actually getting an interview. It means that whatever it is that you have been doing in your job search is working. That's a good feeling, and it's easy to get caught up in the thrill of it all. In your enthusiasm, don't neglect to get the details of the event straight. For example:

- **When is the interview?** Make sure you have the correct day and time noted.

- **Where will the interview be held?** Do you know where the company is actually located? Is it on the other side of town and will you need to fight morning rush hour to get there for a 9:00 a.m. interview? Is the interview located in another city? Will you need to carry your interview clothes with you and change somewhere prior to the interview to prevent the "I've been driving for three hours in the middle of summer" look? Be sure that you factor in any additional time needed to get to the interview punctually.

- **Who will be conducting the interview?** Try to find out as much as possible about the person who will be interviewing you. If you have been doing adequate research on the company, you should have some idea of where this individual fits into the organizational scheme. Having this bit of information can help you prepare better for the questions that may come your way. For example, if your career is highly technical in nature and your first interview with this company is with a representative from the Human Resources department, you might have to change your wording so that this interviewer knows what you're talking about. It might also be the case that you will be interviewed by more than one person at the same time. This presents a different scenario for you. Again, having as much information beforehand as possible can help you better prepare.

Dress for the occasion.

In the military, dressing was easy. You wore your BDUs, Class A's, or dress blues depending upon the occasion. You knew which shoes or boots went with what outfit, and green looked good on everyone. Others in the military could take one look at you while you were wearing your uniform and immediately have an idea of how long you had been in the military, which unit you currently belonged to, and what type of training you'd accomplished. You were, in a manner of thinking, a walking resume.

As a civilian, someone may not be able to read you as carefully on first glance, but impressions will be made right off the bat, and they are not easily changed.

By the time you land your first interview, you will hopefully be well on your way to establishing your civilian wardrobe. Interview outfits, however, sometimes differ from those you would wear on a day-to-day basis. Bottom line: You want to make a good first impression, and you only have one opportunity to do it. *Dress up.*

Let common sense prevail when you select your interview outfit. For example, if you're applying for a managerial or executive-level job, your attire should obviously fit the occasion. If the thought of matching your socks, shoes, shirt, and skirt or pants terrifies you, you may want to employ the services of a professional shopper at a reputable department store.

Say It Isn't So

In my first civilian job, I conducted interviews with mostly people who were transitioning from the military. I had one individual who asked me what he should wear when he came to the interview with me. I told him to wear whatever he thought would be appropriate to interview for a civilian job. He showed up in his BDUs. He did not get the job. Attire was not the only consideration, but it certainly weighed in the decision.

—Dale Michaels, Defense Contractor

Put on a good attitude.

Don't be fooled. Qualifications are important. Looks help. Attitude, however, can make or break your chances. How you come across to potential employers plays an ultra-vital role in the decision-making process. It can distinguish you from others who want the same job.

Of course, different employers seek different characteristics. Suffice it to say, there is not a one-size-fits-all attitude that will work every time. There are specific traits, however, that generally serve you well during such situations.

For example, it usually doesn't hurt to be seen as a team player, a contributor, a leader, and a follower. Perception is reality and you do have the potential to sit in different roles as the needs of your employer require it. This is not to say that you should suck up and be what someone wants you to be just for the sake of acceptance. It is to say that everyone has a boss and you have to fit into an organization. More often than you might think, that "fit" counts more than having hardcore skills or sought-after degrees.

You probably already know that there is a fine line between confidence and arrogance. Keep in mind that the former is a big plus; the latter is not and is often seen as aggressive. In the military, you might have been a bold, audacious, risk-taking warrior. Hoo-ah. Check it at the door before you leave your house and go to your interview.

In some situations, your military rank can help you find substantial employment after the service, such as in the defense contracting arena. In other arenas, however, your old rank just doesn't count anymore regardless of whether you were a private or a general. (In many instances, people won't even know the difference between the two.) The playing field is now leveled, and it's up to you to present your best, your true image. If you associate your personal identity too closely with your former, or soon-to-be former, rank, this truth can hurt. Get over it.

Consider the interviewer's perspective.

You may or may not know who will be interviewing you for a position. This person may be a skilled interviewer, able to fairly and objectively decide whether you are the right candidate for the job. This person may not fall into that category. He or she may be unskilled in the interviewing process and may even be intimidated by your skills, abilities, and experiences. You never know what emotional baggage someone else is carrying, and that someone includes the person who might be sitting across the desk from you at your next interview.

If at all possible, determine who you will be meeting with. Learn what you can about this individual, either through personal contacts or via a company Web site. It may help you present your qualifications in the best light.

Expand your knowledge of the company.

You must already know something about this company because you took the time to give them your resume and/or your job application in the first place. Now it is time to examine your level of knowledge about the organization and to add to it as much as possible. You will want to be able to answer such questions as the following:

- What business is this company really in? Where are their priorities?

- Does the company have good financial fitness?

- Does it have a good reputation within the industry?

- What is the actual size of the company? Where are its offices located?

- Who are the major players in the organization?

- How does the company see itself?

You can gain this type of information a number of different ways. Visit their Web site, if they have one. Obtain a copy of their company profile from any number of corporate directories or registers (i.e., Dun and Bradstreet or Standard and Poor's) available at most libraries. Talk to people you may already know who work for the company. Read the papers or magazines where their name may appear.

The idea here is to know as much about this organization as possible so that you can ask intelligent questions during the interview. An added bonus is, of course, the fact that you will look like you took the time to prepare for the interview itself. It further illustrates the level of your motivation and the type of qualities you could bring to the organization. Employers like that kind of thing. It makes you stand out from others who want the same job.

Practice answering common interview questions.

If there is one thing that you can count on in an interview, it is that no two will be exactly the same. The human element involved will always keep the matter interesting. While you may not know every question that will get thrown at you, you can guess that there will be some generally accepted common questions in the mix.

You should have an idea of how to best answer these questions without sounding like you memorized them the night before. To that end, here is a list of potential questions and comments that may get you thinking about their real meanings and what you'd like to say:

- **Tell me about yourself.** Keep it on a professional level here. Don't talk endlessly on the subject of yourself. You might say more than you really need to at this point. This is a great opportunity to tell the employer about your professional self. For example:

  □ How much experience you have in a given field

  □ Any credentials you have relative to the position

  □ Why you are interested in the position

  □ What you feel you could bring to the company

- **How did you learn about this opportunity?** This will tell the employer how well the company's advertising is doing, assuming the position was an announced one.

- **What do you know about our company?** Your answer to this question will immediately tell the employer whether you are a serious candidate or not. Obviously, you should be able to answer this with some indication of prior research.

- **What qualifies you for this job?** Again, how well you answer this question will show the employer just how much you know about the position.

- **When will you be able to begin working?** Make sure you have a fix on this date before you're asked the question. If you are on permissive TAD/TDY, you are not supposed to start working on someone else's dime as you are still under Uncle Sam's control. If you are on transition leave (formerly known as terminal leave), it is allowable.

- **Would you consider a different job within this company?** Don't be discouraged by this question. You may have come to the company initially with interest in one job. After interviewing you, the employer may feel that you are not right for the job in question, but he or she may want to apply your skills in another area. Keep your mind open. The other job could be a better opportunity.

- **What specific experience have you had in this area?** Review your resume before the interview. It may have been some time since you last gave it a glance. Your interview will be conducted based upon what you included in that document.

- **Why did you leave your last employer? (Why are you looking for a new job?)** Craft your answer to this question with a positive tone. You might say that you felt you had accomplished all you possibly could in your last job and you were now ready for new challenges. If you have negative feelings about your last employer (the military), keep them in check. It's never a good idea to badmouth your past employer in front of a potential new one. While intelligent individuals realize there are two sides to every story, such comments could send the wrong signals unnecessarily. You don't want to be marked as a potential troublemaker.

- **What did you like most about your last job? Least?** Keep whatever you choose to say here also in a positive light. For example, you might say that you least liked the amount of hours needed to complete your tasks. You would balance that dislike, however, by adding that you recognized the need for putting in those hours due to the job requirements at that time (suggesting that you will do what it takes to get the job done).

- **Tell me about your strengths. Your weaknesses?** Some people find it difficult to talk about their strengths and even more difficult to talk about their weaknesses. If you find this tough, get over it. If you don't sell your capabilities, no one else will. If you are asked about your weaknesses, make sure it's a "good" weakness as opposed to the "I always come in late for work" variety. An example of a good weakness might be your never-ending diligence to complete a project.

- **Tell me about a time when you failed.** This may sound like a trick question, but it's not. Everyone has had a less than stellar work experience at some point. If you are asked this or a similar type of question, make sure you show how you overcame your failure. It will show the employer that you're human and learned from your mistakes.

- **Describe your greatest career achievement to date.** Your answer will reveal to the employer what is important to you professionally.

- **Where do you see yourself in one year? In five?** Everyone should have a plan or at least an idea of one. How you answer this will show the employer how organized and visionary your thought processes are in this area.

- **Are you flexible?** This one should be easy for anyone in the military. Not to stereotype here, but flexibility is generally one of the strengths associated with a camouflaged lifestyle.

- **Why should I hire you over others who are just as qualified or even more qualified for this job?** If your resume makes you look good (which it probably did to get you to the interview), then now is the time to walk the talk. This isn't the time to be overly humble and shy. If you want this job, say so and give good reasons for it.

- **What salary are you seeking?** If this is the first interview, defer this question to a later time. Explain that you need to know more about the position and its responsibilities before you can discuss this point.

Know how to handle potentially illegal questions.

Interviewers may either be skilled in the art of interviewing or not. Those who are not will sometimes ask questions in a way, unknowingly or not, that may actually be illegal. For example:

- Were you honorably discharged from the military?

- Do you have any disabilities?

- Are you a U.S. citizen?

- How old are you?

- Are you married?

- How many kids do you have?

- What is your religion?

- Who did you vote for in the last election?

- Have you ever been arrested?

- Are you pregnant?

You may choose to be offended at such questions, or you may decide to explore the intent of the interviewer for better understanding. For example, ask the employer to repeat the question. If the question is stated in the same manner, ask him how that information relates to the position. This is a perfectly acceptable question on your part. You might also try to answer the intent (if there appears to be one) of the question rather than the question itself. For example, *Have you been honorably discharged from the military?* might just mean, "What branch of service did you serve in?" or "What type of education and training did you receive while you were in the military?" Knowing in advance how you would handle such a situation may pay off in a big way for you later.

Show yourself the money—and the benefits.

Your first interview for a particular position may not even address the topic of money and benefits. That's not unusual. You should be prepared for it regardless.

Before you meet with a potential employer, know what type of salary and what types of benefits you are seeking. Having said that, try to avoid the topic on a first interview if at all possible. You want to be sure that you are the right person for the job. You don't necessarily know that five minutes into an interview. If you are forced into the discussion, at least be able to deflect the question back on the interviewer or state your requirement in terms of a salary range versus an exact amount.

Chapter 8, "Evaluating and Negotiating Job Offers," provides more insight into this area.

Prepare your own list of questions.

Remember that the whole point of doing well at an interview is to generate choices for yourself. For this to happen, you have to get information about the company, the job, and the people who work there in addition to sharing information about yourself. That is the only way you can make a genuinely educated decision about the job at a later time.

Here is a sampling of questions that you might consider asking an employer:

- What characteristics are you seeking in an employee for this position?

- If selected for this position, who would I be working with?

- Where is the job located? What are the scheduled work hours?

- Does this position require that I travel? How much?

- Would there be an initial training period?

- What are the goals of this company for the next year? For the next three?

- Is advancement within the company a possibility?

- When and how are performance reviews accomplished?

- Why is this position now open?

- Describe a typical day on the job here.

- Where does this position fit into the organizational food chain?

- What is the working environment like here?

- If hired, what would be the three top issues I would be expected to address?

- What type of salary is typically paid for someone in such a position?

Make up your mind to be yourself.

Sometimes, something strange happens to people who are going to be interviewed. They feel an unnatural need to represent themselves as someone they are not.

You don't want to fall for this line of thinking. Yes, it is certainly important to make a good impression. The last thing you want to do on an interview, however, is present yourself as someone you are not. You must be comfortable in your own skin. That true perception will work far better for you than the "I'm putting on my best face for you, but it's only an act so I can get this job" facade.

A successful interview is just the first step in what is going to be an actual relationship. You will benefit far more from a truthful and realistic beginning than by using the dog-and-pony-show approach. Keep yourself grounded in reality, and you should do just fine.

The Day of and During the Interview

The day of your interview will eventually arrive, and then the fun will begin! The following advice could prove helpful on that long-awaited day.

Arrive on time.

If you want to make a good initial impression, you really can't go wrong with showing up 10 to 15 minutes before your scheduled appointment. Doing so indicates that you had a clue where to show up in the first place. It also gives you an opportunity to check into the nearest restroom for a final once-over of yourself. If you arrive earlier, you run the risk of being "too early." Arriving late is simply not an option. If something terribly unforeseen should happen to cause such a thing, call the employer as soon as possible with an apology and a good reason.

Be a spy.

Don't kid yourself. Your interview may be scheduled to begin at 9:00 a.m. If you arrive in the office (or wherever) at 8:45 a.m., that is when you can consider your interview as having begun. The person who has the power to hire you may not be directly looking at you, but others who have the ear of that person will.

Use this time to the best of your ability. Be polite, sociable, and charming to *everyone*. You never know who has the real authority in an organization. Job titles can be impressive; however, power doesn't necessarily earn the biggest paycheck.

Be cognizant of your body language.

In front of a military board, this can mean you wear an impeccable uniform, your eyes are front and center, your back is erect, and your hands are stiffly at your side. Relax! Civilian interviews may be stressful, but you won't be required to exhibit the same body language. In fact, doing so could even subliminally hurt your chances for serious consideration.

Good body language tips include the following:

- **Be dressed for the occasion.** You want to feel comfortable in your own skin, and an extension of that skin is found in your clothes. If you look good, you feel good. This is half of the "first impression" battle alone. If you feel like you need further guidance in this area, read the section entitled "Dressed for the Occasion" earlier in this chapter.

- **Offer a firm and confident (not bone-crunching or sweaty) handshake.** If you find that you are nervous, casually wipe your palm on your pants leg or skirt before you shake your interviewer's hand.

- **Maintain good posture.** Good posture means sitting straight and leaning a bit forward toward the interviewer to emphasize nonverbal interest in what he or she has to say to you.

- **Maintain good eye contact.** This doesn't mean staring down your future employer. It does mean appearing interested. The eyes, it has often been said, are the window to your soul. Be sure your soul presents itself in a professional and interested manner. It's okay to blink occasionally.

- **Refrain from nervous habits.** Maybe you are a finger or toe tapper. Maybe you continuously twirl a strand of your hair. Maybe you stutter under pressure, nervously (and endlessly) tap your pen against a table, or swivel in a chair that will allow you to do so. Whatever your vice, try to be aware of how annoying it can be during an interview. It takes the attention off of you and your wonderful qualifications and puts it on your distracting defense mechanisms.

Listen.

Listening is a true skill in and of itself. It requires actual concentration on your part, and that isn't always easy to muster when you find yourself in the interview seat. After the interview, you are going to need to fully evaluate the viability of this opportunity. You won't be able to effectively do that if your nerves, excitement, or lack of concentration got in your way. If it helps you, take notes. It's generally acceptable to do this during the interview. Always ask the permission of the person who is conducting the interview first and keep your notes brief but understandable to you later.

If you want the job, ask for it.

If, after what you've learned during the course of the interview, you decide that you would potentially like to have this job, ask for it. You have nothing to lose and only a choice in the matter to gain. Live on the edge.

Look into the future.

Before you leave the interview, it is perfectly acceptable to ask when a selection will be made and when the company would like to see someone sitting in that position. If they can provide this information to you at this point, it will give you a clearer picture of the hiring timeline.

After the Interview

One of the biggest mistakes job seekers make is to fail to follow up. Once the interview is over, you must continue your strategic efforts to obtain the job. You should certainly send a thank-you letter or note. (See Chapter 6, "Creating Effective Job Search Letters," for more information on this topic.) You could also make a follow-up call in a week or so to see how the selection process is progressing. You don't want to stalk the employer, but you want to keep your name fresh in his mind.

Send a thank-you note.

Once, a client of mine at Fort Huachuca, Arizona, reported to me he and another candidate were in final contention for a lucrative job with a major utility company. My client promptly sent a thank-you note following his interview, while the other candidate apparently did not. According to the employer, this small act of common courtesy and professionalism is what made him choose my client over the other one.

Writing or typing up a thank-you note is a simple thing, and yet so many job seekers neglect to do it. Not only does it show that you have good manners, it gives you the opportunity to reinforce your enthusiasm and to remind the employer that your qualifications match his needs perfectly. It also affords you the opportunity to mention anything you might have neglected to mention during the interview.

Don't ignore the potential power of this job search tool. You'll not only make your dear old mum proud, but you just might gain the edge over your competition. To get the best use of this tool, mail it to the person or persons who interviewed you the day of or the day after the interview.

Chapter 6 provides a sample thank-you letter if you find yourself requiring further guidance in this area.

Follow up.

A week or so after sending your thank-you letter, call the person who interviewed you. Make sure they received your note of thanks and reiterate your interest in the position. If you don't already have an answer to the timeframe-for-selection question from the interview, inquire about it now.

The whole idea behind the concept of follow-up strategy is to keep your name fresh in the mind of the employer. You are a potential candidate. You are the best candidate. You need to make sure the employer knows that you feel this way.

There's nothing wrong about being persistent. If you want the job, you need to make your best effort to get it. That means you don't sit around waiting for fate to reward you. You get out there and try your best to influence fate so that you will have the job you want or the choices you desire.

Continue your job search efforts.

You might want the job you interviewed for more than anything else in the world. Great. If you've done everything right and if the moon and the stars are all aligned, you might very well just be waiting for the perfect offer itself. But…if your luck is off by one iota, you need to continue your job search efforts. Dare I remind you of the cliché, "Don't put all your eggs into one basket"? If you've ever gone house hunting, this concept will be crystal clear to you.

Focus on the Family

Nothing is more frustrating than feeling like you have to settle for what's available in the job market. As a family member who may have moved frequently with your active-duty soldier, sailor, or marine, you are probably more than familiar with the concept of "settling." Now is the time to stop settling. There will be no more transfers to some post located in the middle of nowhere, where jobs seem nonexistent. You will no longer have to craft an answer to the inquiring, if not illegal, "How long are you planning to live here?" question often asked by potential employers who suspect that the military will whisk you away once you are adequately trained on the job. As a family member, you now find yourself at the threshold of a new place in your own career path. Maybe it's time for your spouse to follow you around. Maybe it's time for you to rethink your own professional goals and plot a new chart for reaching them. This is not just another transfer time. This is a new beginning. Full speed ahead!

CHAPTER 8 Evaluating and Negotiating Job Offers

If you thought going to the interview was a thrill, wait until you are actually offered a job! This is where the real decision work comes into play and stress levels can go way up. This is particularly true if you have more than one offer to evaluate.

You could panic and let your fear direct all the decisions to be made regarding your immediate future. This is not an uncommon occurrence. Fear of the unknown is the genuine article, and it often seems easier to accept the first job offered than to wait for other offers that may be soon in coming. After all, bills have to be paid and children must be fed and clothed.

It takes great personal courage to wait it out for the right opportunity. Only you can judge your timeline here. As you begin your analysis of a particular offer or of multiple offers, take comfort in the fact that if you accept a job and find that you don't like it (or they don't like you), the world will not end. You will simply have to find another job. If you have the skills to prepare and conduct a job search, you can accomplish that task without fail at any given time. Portability. Mobility. Ability. These aren't unfamiliar skills for anyone who has served in the U.S. military.

One word of caution here: Be sure you really have an offer before you begin to evaluate it. If what you have is verbal banter, get it in writing. Most companies will extend their offers to potential candidates in writing. It protects them and it protects you. If you're dealing with a company that has made a verbal offer to you and they are waiting for your acceptance or declination, put the terms discussed in writing yourself and secure their signatures on the document. Extreme? Perhaps, but it's better that way. Don't worry about offending anyone. This is business and they will understand.

Evaluating the Offer

Once you have been offered a position, you can assume that a company *wants* to hire you. The proverbial ball is now in your court and it's up to you to decide whether you want to play the game.

It may be helpful to look at the offer from two different angles. First, do you really want the job? Second, can you and the employer come to an acceptable compensation package?

Do you really want the job?

Clearly you want a job or you wouldn't be subjecting yourself to this whole gut-wrenching process. In the heat of the moment, however, don't make the mistake of accepting just any job. Accept the one that is right for you and your family.

Now is the time to carefully examine all the information you have gathered, from all sources, about the company and about the job itself. Put that information to the test now. The following Job Offer Initial Evaluation Checklist will enable you to effectively evaluate up to three job offers at once.

After each interview, take the time to review the list and address the points listed. Go a step further and look at the list *before* you go to the interview to be sure all those points are covered.

If you receive multiple offers, you may consider yourself fortunate or tortured. In either event, multiple offers are a reality, and one that is better to find yourself in than its opposite. The following Comparison Matrix may assist you if you find yourself comparing apples and oranges.

Job Offer Initial Evaluation Checklist

Factor	A	B	C
(Check the block to indicate a "yes." Leave blank for "no.")			
Have an actual job offer in writing for a position	☐	☐	☐
Have informed employer when decision will be made	☐	☐	☐
Possess a clear understanding of the actual work responsibilities	☐	☐	☐
Skills and abilities are a match for those responsibilities	☐	☐	☐
Know where this job fits on an organizational level	☐	☐	☐
Know who would be immediate supervisor	☐	☐	☐
Opportunity supports overall career goals	☐	☐	☐
Employer has a good industry reputation	☐	☐	☐
Employee turnover rate is low at this company	☐	☐	☐
Job security appears to exist	☐	☐	☐
Satisfied with the actual job location	☐	☐	☐
Relocation a possibility at some point	☐	☐	☐
Travel a possibility	☐	☐	☐
Comfortable with the stated work schedule	☐	☐	☐
Training and development opportunities exist	☐	☐	☐
Internal/external advancement possibilities exist	☐	☐	☐
Competitive base salary being offered	☐	☐	☐
Adequate benefits package offered	☐	☐	☐
Know how often salary reviews conducted	☐	☐	☐
Understand company policy on cost-of-living factor	☐	☐	☐
Know how often performance reviews are conducted	☐	☐	☐

Comparison Matrix

Complete one sheet for each job and then compare the numbers. Use this rating scale:

    0 = Doesn't Apply

    1 = Unacceptable

    2 = Acceptable

    3 = Highly Acceptable

    4 = Outstanding

Factor	0	1	2	3	4
Competitive salary					
Comprehensive benefits package					
Signing bonus and/or other perks					
Position level within company					
Skills a good match for qualifications					
Advancement opportunities					
Company reputation					
Work environment					
Corporate culture similar to own					
Job location / Commute Time					
Work schedule a personal fit					
Travel requirements acceptable					
Job appears to have security					
Subtotal					
TOTAL SCORE FOR THIS OFFER					

Photocopy the sheet on page 160 for each job you are considering. Using the legend provided at the top of the form, assign a score for each of the listed items. After you've plugged in all the numbers for each item on the list, add the totals. Do this for each position you are considering and then compare the numbers between the jobs. The numbers won't lie. The job prospect having the highest score will represent the one that has most of the characteristics you have deemed important. Only you can decide, however, if it is the job you will actually select.

Can you and the employer come to an acceptable compensation package?

Certainly salary is a big deal. In our ever so superficial society, it is how we keep score professionally. You may or may not subscribe to that line of thinking, but the facts are still there. The higher the salary offered, the more enticing the job sounds.

It's important to remember, though, that the total compensation package is not made up of salary alone. It includes salary plus benefits. You need to evaluate the whole package and not just the base dollar figure.

Show Me the Money: Salary Expectations vs. Salary Realities

Anyone who has ever thought about transitioning from the military has heard the story about the young soldier, sailor, airman, or marine who left the military after his first tour was up only to be hired by a company that offered him the elusive 100K job.

I won't say that this has never happened before, but it is certainly not the norm. The truth in the matter often gets exaggerated with each telling. The reality depends upon a number of factors. What career field are you targeting and how much marketable experience do you have in it? Where are you physically targeting a job? Cost-of-living surveys say that salaries are higher in metropolitan areas than in the middle of nowhere. If you don't believe that, go online and see for yourself. Check out www.salary.com or www.homefair.com and do a little comparison shopping. You'll be amazed. Certain parts of the country

161

demand higher wages than other parts simply because of cost-of-living differences. Some companies, however, have established their pay structures based on national rather than regional averages. They do this because it facilitates the transfer of employees internally without the continual need for salary adjustments. How do you find out? Ask the employer. Once you have been offered a job, the door is wide open for discussing all the finer details, from salary to benefits.

The bottom line is that you want to be paid competitively for what your skills and experiences are worth in the marketplace. Note here that I didn't say "what you are worth." As tempting as it may be, do not equate your personal worth with any salary figure being offered to you. They are two distinct issues, and clouding them will only promote an unhealthy mental attitude for the long run.

Salary negotiation should be an area where everyone wins. You and the employer should both walk away from a successful negotiation process feeling professionally pleased. Knowing when to feel this way, however, can be dubious at best. What you need to do, before you ever find yourself at an interview, is research the topic as much as possible. Know what someone in your career field, working in the location(s) you are targeting and sharing your level of expertise, makes.

You may have to be creative to find out this type of information as the subject of salaries earned is not as open a topic as in the military. In fact, in some companies discussing the topic with other employees could be grounds for dismissal. On the other hand, some employers readily publish their pay scales. To locate such information try the following:

- Research any number of national, state, and/or industry-specific salary surveys available on the Internet or through your local library.
  - □ Business publications, trade associations, and professional organizations usually publish annual salary surveys.

- □ Consult the U.S. Department of Labor's Occupational Outlook Handbook online at http://stats.bls.gov.

- Utilize cost-of-living and salary calculators available online at reputable Web sites. Two to check out are

  - □ www.salary.com

  - □ www.homefair.com

- Study want ads of online job banks and in newspapers, which often list salary ranges.

  - □ One good online source is www.newspapers.com.

  - □ Talk discreetly to others you know who might have an idea of such information.

Salary Negotiation Basics and Tips

If you have effectively researched salary norms that may apply to you, then you are at the point where you can plan a realistic negotiation campaign. Such a campaign involves having a genuine understanding about negotiation basics. Keep in mind that you and the employer should agree on the following:

- What the responsibilities are for the job you are being offered

- What the going rate is for such a position in the current market

- What you are being offered, salary-wise, for this position by the company

- How future salary increases are calculated

The process will end in one of four ways:

1. You get the salary you want when you ask for it.

2. You get part of the salary you want.

3. You accept the offered salary as is.

4. The company withdraws the offer.

It would be to your advantage to know before the process begins how comfortable you see yourself with each ending. Only you can set the risk level for yourself.

Here are some additional tips regarding the salary negotiation process:

- Be able to express your salary requirements in any terms such as annual, monthly, weekly, daily, and even per minute.

- Let the employer bring up the subject of compensation first. It usually isn't a topic of discussion until after you've been offered a job.

- Remember, you are in the best position to negotiate *before* you actually accept a job.

- If you are asked what your salary requirements are early in the interview, defer your answer until you have learned more about the responsibilities of the position. Some employers use this tactic to screen out candidates having unacceptable salary ranges.

- Some employers request a salary history for additional use as a screening tool. They want to know what you've worked for in the past so that they can base future offers on that amount. Avoid providing this kind of information if at all possible. Theoretically, you want to be offered more than you've been making. Indeed, the military isn't famous for its high-paying jobs. Skills and expertise that you've acquired while in uniform, however, can be a totally different story. If you are asked for salary information, explain to the employer that, no offense intended, but you would rather discuss the current position in light of its qualifications and your match for them. Realize of course that not providing such information could result in a withdrawal of an offer. If you agree to provide an employer with a salary history, an example of one is provided for you below. Be sure you provide the "salary" from the military that includes the cost of your benefits as well. If you don't know what that is, contact your finance office for more information.

James Johnson

555 Overlook Place, Dulles, VA 55555 (555)571-5555

Salary History

Job Title	Employer	Annual Salary
Satellite Network Engineer	U.S. Army	$65,000
Operations Manager	U.S. Army	$57,000
Personnel Supervisor	U.S. Army	$50,000
Communications Technician	U.S. Army	$45,000

- If you are asked what your salary requirements are after learning more about the job, answer the question with a question. For example:

   Employer: Tell me, what type of salary are you seeking?

   Job seeker: What range of salary are you willing to pay for this position?

   Don't play verbal Ping-Pong on the issue. If you must be the first to come up with a range, add at least 10 to 15 percent onto the highest end of your acceptable salary range.

- Be realistic. Understand that employers usually have a salary range that they can honestly offer. You will either like that range or not. Make a counteroffer if you are not satisfied with the one put before you. If you still can't get to that happy meeting point, be willing to say thanks but no thanks and walk away.

- Couple your counteroffer with reasons why your skills are worth the extra money.

- Realize that once an offer is made to you, it is only the beginning of the negotiation process. It is perfectly acceptable to ask for more once an offer has been made. You will either get what you ask for or not.

- Remember that benefits and perks are also negotiable.

- Provide suggestions to the employer if necessary.

- Realize that the salary you accept will more than likely represent the basis for your future salaries.

- Be prepared to back up any requests for a high salary with solid supporting facts. You should be paid more because _____ (you fill in the blank).

- Maintain a positive and professional attitude throughout the process. How you negotiate your own salary and benefits may suggest to the employer how you will perform on the job. There is no reason to be confrontational. Cooperation is key.

- Ask the employer about the company's salary review policy. Perhaps you can also negotiate a raise at a future date. Inquire about salary increases as well.

- Inquire about the availability of a severance package.

- Don't accept or reject an offer immediately once it has been made. Ask for a day or two to think it over.

Benefits and Perks: The Other Half of the Salary Picture

Benefits and perks are just as important in a compensation package as the base salary and may be negotiated as such. It would be to your advantage to first settle on the salary portion and then examine the benefits and perks as additional items.

Following is a brief list of potential benefits to consider aside from the basic offered salary.

Financial-Related Benefits

Commissions

- In addition to your base salary, are commissions available? What is the percentage? This is usually a possibility if you work in sales or business development.

Sign-on Bonus

- Keep in mind that signing bonuses are taxed as regular income.

Performance Bonus

- Does the company offer one? Are there other types of compensation such as a year-end bonus?

Relocation Allowances

- If accepting a position involves any type of commute, you may be offered an additional incentive for such travel time.

- If a major move is involved with your acceptance of a job, be sure to inquire about any additional assistance potentially available to you. Depending upon your level of employment, you might find that a company is willing to pay for any expenses you incur as a result of selling or purchasing a new home. Some companies will even cover the cost of your new driver's license, necessary utility hookups, or even employment assistance for your spouse.

Financial Planning and Tax Assistance

- Some companies, particularly if you are working abroad for them, will provide such services.

Expense Account

- Does the company offer an account to cover the cost of your work-related expenses? This might be an issue of high importance if you work out of your home for them. In such a case, your personal rent or mortgage might be considered a business expense as well as your telephone, Internet service, and automobile.

Paid Time Off

Vacation/Sick/Personal Days

- How much leave can be earned and on what schedule? For example, you may only be eligible for one week of vacation and only after having worked for the company for a specific length of time. Generally, the longer you work for a firm, the more vacation days you are allowed. A word of advice, though: Go ahead and mourn the loss of the annual 30 days of leave you received in the military. You probably won't be seeing that again. Some companies will offer vacation, sick, and personal days. Others may just offer a set number of days and you fit your vacation, doctor appointments, and other errands into them however you want.

Funeral/Bereavement

- Most firms will offer you up to three days of paid leave to attend the funeral of an immediate family member.

Legal Obligations

- If you must obligate to serving time in the Reserves, find out if the employer supports this in practice as he should by law.

- Employers are also obligated to allow you paid time to perform jury duty.

Health, Dental, and Vision Insurance

In the military, when you or someone in your immediate family needed to see a doctor, you called the dispensary or the military hospital and usually made a same-day appointment. Unless you incurred an overnight stay, you generally walked away from that visit without a bill. That is not necessarily what will happen to you as a civilian.

As you consider the health, dental, and vision insurance benefits offered to you, make sure you understand the answer to these questions:

- How much will each of these benefits actually cost you?

- When does coverage begin?

- Will you have flexibility to change any selected policies at a later time?

- Do you have flexibility in designing your own plans?

- What happens to your coverage should you leave the company?

- Do you or your family have any pre-existing medical conditions you need to consider?

Life Insurance
- Is this a company-paid benefit?

- What is the cost of additional coverage for yourself or family members, if available?

401(k)
- Are matching funds by the company offered? If so, at what percentage?

- What are the contribution limits?

- When are you considered fully vested in the program?

Stock Options
- Is there a discount available for purchase of company stock?

- Are you allowed to buy and sell?

- Is there a commission fee?

Education and Training
- Is tuition assistance available for you or family members?

- How is the program managed? Are initial out-of-pocket expenses a possibility?

- Are memberships in professionally related organizations/ associations paid for by the company?

Personal Care

- Examples of such benefits may include subsidized or on-site child care, elder care, fitness facilities, or other similar items.

Work-Related Benefits

Flexible Work Schedules and Telecommuting

- Depending upon the nature of your employment, you may have the opportunity to adjust your work hours or to work out of your home. If these possibilities interest you, be sure to inquire about them during your interview.

Severance Package

- The last thing you are probably thinking about as you consider a new job is what would happen if you lost your job. Considering the subject of a severance package hardly seems like a positive thing to do, but in the event it actually happens, you will be endlessly happy that you did think about it. Not all companies will offer this and there is no standard package, but it doesn't hurt to ask.

Perks

- Are you eligible for any additional perks such as a company-paid cell phone, automobile, or credit card?

Making the Decision: Using Your Gut

Knowing how to effectively establish a realistic salary range and negotiate the base salary plus benefits will do you no good unless you can come to a decision. The last phase of any negotiation process is the ultimate moment where you need to actually accept or decline a job.

Timing is critical and you have to be willing to either accept a job with the caveats discussed in this chapter or you need to be able to walk away and not look back. In other words, it's show time and you have to play.

In the end, if you are offered a position, only you can decide whether to accept it. You should listen to your gut instincts because they will rarely steer you in the wrong direction. Unfortunately, you don't have the benefit of looking into a crystal ball to see if you are making the right decision for the long run. You'll just have to look at the facts, trust your instincts, and take your chances. The worst thing that will happen is that you make the wrong decision and end up looking for another job. The world will not stop spinning; life will go on.

You now know how to conduct an effective job search and you will use those skills throughout your post-military professional life.

Focus on the Family

Everyone likes to feel that he or she earns a decent salary that truly matches one's level of competency. Too often, as a mobile military family member, that concept has been more of an enigma than a reality. If you have found that your skills, experiences, and talents have been financially shortchanged because of the locations you have lived in, now is the time to breathe a sigh of relief. You and your spouse now have a real choice in deciding where you want to live and work. There are many factors to consider as you both ponder where your next home should be. If salary is indeed a driving force, go for it! Consider, however, all aspects of potential offers. High salaries for either of you is great. What waits on the flip side of a high paycheck, however? Long working hours. Extensive responsibility. Limited time at home. (Almost sounds like life in the military, doesn't it?) Salary is but one aspect of your transition. Whether you are evaluating your next salary or your spouse's, view the offers holistically and not just in terms of dollars and cents.

CHAPTER 9 You're Hired. Now What?

Congratulations! You're hired, happy, and soon to receive your first paycheck. Life is good. Keep it good by realizing a few cold, hard facts.

This is not the perfect job, even though you may initially believe it to be so. Eventually, the honeymoon will end and reality will rear its ugly head. It may be a job you genuinely like and one that provides great opportunity for you to advance or to do whatever is important to you. It is, however, another step in your professional life, and it will not be without its ups and downs. Enjoy the euphoria, but don't be surprised when it ends. It's at that point that your true colors on the job will show.

Wise Words of Advice for Adjusting to Life on the Job as a Civilian

Face it. You're now the new kid on the block, and it would be to your distinct advantage to heed the following guidance as you begin your new job.

Stop. Look. Listen. Learn.

You may have known it all in your last job, but this is not that job. Despite what may be your level of expertise in a particular career field, you are still the new person in the company and have a thing or two to learn. Don't be too hard on yourself in the beginning. Make an effort to observe how people in your company interact with one another. Let others around you get to know you a bit as well. Your environment has changed for sure, but so has theirs. This is the start of a new relationship for all involved. It will no doubt be a good one, but don't expect it to be bump-free.

Remember the Good

When you start your new job, remember the good attributes that the military taught you about being at the appointed place at the appointed time, manners, respect, sense of urgency, etc. Forget, however, the hoo-ah military jargon, and don't be over-aggressive.

—Dale Michaels, Defense Contractor

Don't try to change the company your first week on the job.

You will of course have your mark to make. Depending upon the nature of your new position, you might want to consider holding on to that thought for a few months.

The typical military fashion of walking in and changing everything to your grand vision may not be as welcome in the civilian world as it was accepted in the military world. If you insist on changing everything your first month on the job, you may find yourself not well liked within the organization by your peers or even your supervisors. In essence, you are nonverbally communicating to them that they haven't had a clue and have been doing business wrong all along.

Your grand vision may indeed be the correct direction for the company, but give it time. Earn your credibility first, and then you may have ample opportunity to do whatever you want.

Changes

Don't try to make changes too fast. The civilian world is not used to it, at least in the job I had.

—Laurie Davis, Women's Health Consultant

Don't participate in office gossip—yet.

It happens in every office. You know all about it already. Gossip runs rampant in the military as well. If you have the skill necessary to filter out the fluff from the fact, gossip can be an invaluable, unofficial management tool. Listen to it, but avoid adding your two cents at this time. If you are new to the organization and don't have established relationships with everyone already, gossiping can backfire on you in a heartbeat. Make it a point to stay above the fray at this time. Professional alliances made too early may disadvantage you later. Get to know everyone on equal footing and give them the same opportunity with you.

Be considerate of your new colleagues.

If you avoid trying to change everything in the beginning and avoid the gossip machine, then you are being considerate of your new colleagues. Take it a step further and consider the not-so-obvious elements as well. If you drink coffee and there is a coffee fund, contribute. If everyone meets for lunch once a week, make an effort to join them. These are examples of seemingly insignificant events that, in the long run, make a group of people a team. You know this from wearing a uniform. It is the same without the rank on as well.

Take It Easy

The civilians that I have worked with are very laid back compared to being in the military. No one is in a rush or trying to stay busy. It's a different mind set.

—Steve Martin, Technical Instructor, General Dynamics

Don't feel like a task is beneath your level of expertise.

If you were lucky enough to have an administrative assistant in the military, he or she might have made those photocopies for you or booked your hotel room for your business trips. You may or may not have that same luxury as a civilian. In any event, realize that you may very well be the one to do the grunt work at some point whether you like it or not.

Make yourself indispensable.

Learn everything you possibly can and be of assistance to anyone who needs it. By making yourself indispensable, you build a power base that may span varying levels of responsibility, and that is a good base to build. Power, within an organization, doesn't necessarily rest with the person holding the most impressive job title or making the most bucks. It rests with the person who is well connected, knowledgeable, available, and willing to contribute. You want to be that person or be best friends with that person.

Keep your eyes open for your next job.

It may sound counterproductive to suggest that you look for your next job once you've begun your new one. It's not.

In the military, you had a career path opportunity. Maybe you enlisted or were commissioned and chose that path from beginning to retirement. Maybe you joined the military and figured out that it wasn't where you wanted to be forever. Either way, the structure of that path was there. You punched the right tickets and you theoretically progressed.

It is not always as cut-and-dry in the civilian workplace. You are the one who has to chart your career path. You may be lucky enough to have individuals on your side to assist you in this area, but the majority of the responsibility for its success depends upon you. The bottom line here is that you need to always keep your eyes open for the next step. It may be one that exists within the new company you have selected or it may not. You may not even consider leaving your current job for years to come or you may bail at the first opportunity. You would be doing yourself a career favor, however, to be aware of what's out there periodically. Business can change on a dime. If you don't have the proverbial "Plan B," you might find yourself at a significant disadvantage.

Keep your skills current.

Planning for future opportunities will do you no good unless you have the skills necessary to compete for those jobs. Likewise, success in your current position will demand that you keep up-to-date on the required competencies. Investigate training opportunities in your new organization. Take advantage of every bit of learning available to you. Explore self-directed opportunities as well. Maybe it's time to examine your academic history and improve upon it. Take this one piece of your professional self and put it under a microscope. What condition is it in now and how can it be improved? Maintaining and enhancing your skills will benefit the goals of the organization and your own personal goals as well.

Be willing to admit to a mistake.

Every accepted opportunity deserves a fair chance. If you have given this one its chance and you still feel that it was the wrong decision, be willing to admit that to yourself and move on. If you do not wish to remain in the job you accepted, then discreetly begin your job search process over again. No one should be unhappy in their job. You spend more time at work than you do at home on the average. Make those hours count.

Keep your resume updated.

You may never want to see a resume again. Sorry about that! It would be to your advantage, however, to periodically review your resume and update it. You will find it a far easier task than being forced into time-crunching total rewrites at some future point. Opportunities come and go in the blink of an eye in business. If you want to remain competitive in your field, you must have the ability to respond to changing events in a timely fashion. Keeping your credentials updated on a diskette or on your hard drive is a good idea.

You're Not in Kansas Anymore

I remember my first day as a civilian. I needed to sign for some equipment from another unit. The First Sergeant said we could borrow it, but that he needed "a soldier" to come and sign for it. Talk about a reality check. The hardest thing for me about leaving the military was losing that inherent trust that comes with the uniform and having to start over earning a reputation as a civilian.

—Tom Wiederstein, DOD UAV Instructor

In Conclusion...

You know that you're not the first person to ever transition from the military in search of a civilian job. It may, however, be the first time *you* have ever faced such an obstacle, and that makes it relevant to you and your family.

Everybody who has gone through this process before has his or her own unique story to tell, just as you will too. You may look back on your transition with mixed emotions. It is, after all, a bittersweet time in your career and in your life. Either by choice or by force, you are closing the door on one part of your life and opening another one that doesn't always provide a clear picture of what to expect. The unknown can be daunting to say the least. Your experience while in uniform may have been a good one or not. That depends on how you chose to experience it, just as your transition depends on how you choose to experience it.

To the Future

I look forward to starting my life after the military. Picture your military career as a glass of water that is midway filled. One can look at the glass and say it is half empty and dwell on the promotion list that you didn't come out on or the job you didn't get or the performance rating that you didn't get that you felt you deserved. I'd rather look at that glass as half full, and look at what water can still go into it. I'm excited about the future and I have a big smile on my face.

—Michael L. Holley, US Army, LTC, Retired

There's no doubt that you won't always have control over the circumstances or the opportunities that may or may not come your way. What you will have control over, however, is how you approach them. Those who have successfully transitioned before you have done so with an open mind. They allowed themselves the luxury of considering all the alternatives, good and bad. They did not rush decisions that required careful consideration. They asked relevant questions of potential employers and others having knowledge they required. They researched all aspects of the job opportunities using current literature. They listened to what others had to say and then made their decisions based upon what was right and beneficial to themselves and their families, regardless of what others might have said or thought.

Just because an opportunity seems to be perfect, doesn't mean it is perfect for *you*. It takes great personal courage to filter out the well-meaning voices of those around you and to listen to your own gut. In the end, it is you who will be waking up every day to go to a job you have chosen to accept. You owe it to yourself and your family to be content with your choice. Make a decision. Give it a fighting chance. Do your best. If, after giving it your best shot, you find that it's not working out, have the sustained courage to look for a new job. You have the tools, the knowledge, and experience in doing so already.

Here's to your glass of water. May it be filled with the best of professional and personal experiences for many years to come.

Focus on the Family

You may not be the only one starting a new job in the family. Now that you have an office to call your home away from home, your spouse may also be in the same situation or knee-deep in the job search process itself. If this is the case, remember to return the consideration and support that you were given during your personal career transition. What goes around, comes around!

APPENDIX | Career Transition Resources

Career Decision Making

America's Career InfoNet
www.acinet.org/acinet

Career Guide to Industries
www.bls.gov/oco/cg/

Career Planning at About.com
www.careerplanning.about.com

DOD Dictionary of Military Terms
www.dtic.mil/doctrine/jel/doddict

JobStar
www.jobstar.org

Occupational Outlook Handbook
www.stats.bls.gov/oco/

*O*NET Dictionary of
Occupational Titles*
www.onetcenter.org

The Riley Guide
www.rileyguide.com

Salary.com
www.salary.com

Salaryexpert.com
www.salaryexpert.com

Wages, Earning & Benefits Data
www.stats.bls.gov

Wall Street Journal **Job Services**
www.careerjournal.com

Education

CollegeNET
www.collegenet.com

Federal Children Scholarship Fund
www.fedscholarships.org

GI Bill Information
www.gibill.va.gov

U.S. Dept of Education
www.ifap.ed.gov

Employer Research

Annual Reports
www.annualreportservice.com

BizWeb
www.bizweb.com

Business.com
www.business.com

CEO Express
www.ceoexpress.com

Chambers of Commerce
www.chambers.com

Corporate Information
www.corporateinformation.com

The Corporate Library
www.thecorporatelibrary.com

D&B Million Dollar Database
www.dnbmdd.com/mddi

Forbes Lists
www.forbes.com/lists

Fortune 500
www.fortune.com

Hoovers Online
www.hoovers.com

Internetnews.com
http://stocks.internetnews.com

Moody's
www.moodys.com

Newspapers USA
www.newspapers.com

Standard & Poors
http://www.standardandpoors.com

Thomas Regional
www.thomasregional.com

Thomas Register
www.thomasregister.com

Family

Air Force Crossroads
www.afcrossroads.com

Army Community & Family
Support Center
www.armymwr.com

Army One Source (AOS)
www.ArmyOneSource.com

Army Well-Being Liaison Office
www.aflo.org

Lifelines Quality of Life Mall
www.lifelines.navy.mil

Marine Corps One Source
www.usmc.mil

Military Assistance Program
(MAP)
http://dod.mil/mapsite

Military.Com
www.military.com

Federal Employment

Army Civilian Personnel Online
(CPO)
www.cpol.army.mil

Dept. of Army Civilian Jobs—
Europe
www.chrma.hqusarer.army.mil

Determine VRA Eligibility
www.chrma.hqusareur.army.mil

Federal Jobs Classifications
www.opm.gov/fedclass/html/
gsseries.htm

Federal Jobs Salary Information
www.opm.gov/oca/payrates

FedWorld
www.fedworld.gov

MWR Jobs Online
www.mwrjobs.army.mil

The Job Page
www.thejobpage.gov

The Resume Place
www.resume-place.com

U.S. Air Force Civilian Jobs
www.afpc.randolph.af.mil

USA Jobs
www.usajobs.opm.gov

U.S. Navy and Marine Corps
Civilian Jobs
www.donhr.navy.mil

Veterans Employment
Opportunities Act
www.opm.gov/veterans

Veterans Preference Q & A
www.dol.gov/elaws/vetspref.htm

Health Care

Deployment Health Support
www.deploymentlink.osd.mil

Retiree Delta Dental Plan
www.ddpdelta.org

Tricare
www.tricare.osd.mil

United Concordia Dental Plan
www.ucci.com

Job Links—Civilian

America's Job Bank
www.ajb.dni.us

Brassring.com
www.brassring.com

CareerBuilder
www.careerbuilder.com

Career.com
www.career.com

Cool Jobs
www.cooljobs.com

Employment Guide.com
www.employmentguide.com

Job-Hunt.org
www.job-hunt.org

Job Monkey
www.jobmonkey.com

JobWeb
www.jobweb.com

Monster.com
www.monster.com

NationJob
www.nationjob.com

Legislative/Government Agencies

Tax Information
www.irs.gov

U.S. Department of Labor
www.dol.gov/vets/

U.S. Federal Government Agencies Directory
(Louisiana State University)
www.lib.lsu.edu/gov/fedgov.html

U.S. House of Representatives
www.house.gov

U.S. Postal Service
www.usps.gov

U.S. Senate
www.senate.gov

U.S. State Department
www.state.gov/

Military Associations

Armed Forces Benefit Association
www.afba.com

Association of the U.S. Army (AUSA)
www.ausa.org

Enlisted Association of National Guard
www.eangus.org

The Military Coalition
www.themilitarycoalition.org/

Military Officers Association
www.moaa.org

Military Family Association
www.nmfa.org/

National Guard
www.ngaus.org

Reserve Officers Association
www.roa.org

Military Compensation and Benefits
Military Pay and Entitlements
www.dfas.mil/money

Personal Benefits Center
www.military.com

Social Security Retirement Planner
www.ssa.gov/retire2/

Thrift Savings Plan
www.tsp.gov

Military Transition Related
AARTS Transcript (DA Form 5454-R)
http://aarts.leavenworth.army.mil

Army Career & Alumni Program
www.acap.army.mil

COOL
www.armyeducation.army.mil/cool

DOD Job Search
http://dod.jobsearch.org

DOD Transportal
www.dodtransportal.org

GOV Benefits
www.govbenefits.gov

Green to Gray
www.greentogray.com

MilitaryHire.com
www.militaryhire.com

Retiree Handbook
www.1perscom.army.mil

Transition Assistance Online (Times Publishing)
www.taonline.com

VetGuide
www.opm.gov/employ/html/vetguide.htm

VetJobs.com
www.vetjobs.com

VMET (DD Form 2586)
www.dmdc.osd.mil/vmet

News
Air Force News
www.af.mil/news/

Army News
www.dtic.mil/armylink/news/

Pentagon News
www.defenselink.mil/news/

Relocation Assistance
National Association of Realtors
www.homefair.com

SITES
http://dmdc.osd.mil

Self-Employment
All Business
www.allbusiness.com

Business Opportunities Handbook
www.ezines.com

Small Business Administration
www.sba.gov

The Small Business Advisor
www.isquare.com

Franchise Opportunities Guide
www.franchise.org

Frannet
www.frannet.com

World Franchising
www.worldfranchising.com

Service Agencies

Air Force Aid Society
www.afas.org

American Red Cross
http://redcross.org

Armed Forces YMCA
http://asymca.org

Army Emergency Relief
http://aerhg.org

Navy-Marine Corps Relief Society
www.nmcrs.org

World USO
http://uso.org

Veterans and Retirees

American Legion
www.legion.org

Arlington National Cemetery
www.arlingtoncemetery.org

Cemetery Administration
www.cem.va.gov

Gulf War Veterans Information
www.gulflink.osd.mil

Retired Military Almanac
www.militaryhandbooks.com

U.S. Retirement Services
www.odcsper.army.mil

Veterans Affairs
www.va.gov

Veterans of Foreign Wars
www.vfw.org

Veterans News & Info Service
www.vnis.com

Voter Information

Federal Voting Assistance Program
www.fvap.gov

Register to Vote Online
http://beavoter.com

U.S. Military Components

Air Force
www.af.mil

Air Force Reserve
www.afreserve.com/home3.asp

Air National Guard
www.ang.af.mil

Air Reserve Personnel Center
http://arpc.afrc.af.mil/subjects.htm

Army
www.army.mil

Army National Guard
www.arng.army.mil

Army Reserve Personnel Center
www.2xcitizen.usar.army.mil/

Army Reserve
www.army.mil/usar/

Coast Guard
www.uscg.mil

Coast Guard Reserve
www.uscg.mil

Employer Support of the Guard & Reserve
www.esgr.org

Guard Family
www.guardfamily.org

Guard Net
www.guardnet.net/

Marine Corps Reserve
www.marforres.usmc.mil

Marine Corps
www.usmc.mil

National Guard Bureau
www.ngb.army.mil

Naval Reserve
www.navres.navy.mil/navresfor/

Naval Reserve Personnel Center
www.nrpc.nola.navy.mil

Navy
www.navy.mil

Reserve Affairs
www.defenselink.mil/ra/

The Virtual Armory
www.virtualarmory.com

USCG Human Resource Center
www.uscg.mil/HQ/HRSIC/RMP/

INDEX

A

activity log checklist, 69
addressees on cover letters, 127
adjustment to civilian jobs, 173–174
administrative tasks in civilian jobs, 175–176
advertisements, 1, 81–83
Air Force, 28
allowances, relocation, 167
appearance/grooming, 16, 142–143, 153
Army
    Career and Alumni Program, 28
    education transcripts, 38
assertiveness, 67
assessments, skills, 15, 38
attitude during interviews, 86, 143–144

B

benefits and compensation, 160, 166–170, 184
    burial, 59
    disability, 45–46, 55–56
    education and training, 38–39, 52–53, 169, 181
    employment, 57
    family and survivor, 58–59
    health and life insurance, 39–41, 57–58
    home loans, 54–55
    life insurance, 39–41, 53–54, 169
    states, 59–60
    unemployment, 25, 42
    veterans, 24, 43, 47
    vocational rehabilitation, 57
body language during interviews, 153–154
bonus, 167
budgeting, 41
burial benefits, 59

C

calculators, online, 35
capitalization on resumes, 123
career decision making Web sites, 181
Certificate of Release Form or Discharge from Active Duty Form (DD 214), 25, 47–48
certification and licensing, 38, 60–61, 121
chambers of commerce, 83
change-of-address cards, 48

checklists
    activity log, 69
    job offer initial evaluation,
        159
    master career catalog,
        72–78
    preseparation counseling
        (DD 2648), 29–31
    preseparation timeline
        activities, 13–26
chronological resumes, 104–106
Civil Service Preference, 59
civilian jobs
    adjustment, 173–174
    administrative tasks,
        175–176
    family and spouse issues,
        179–180
    Web sites, 183
clothing allowance, 56
co-workers in the military, 5
Coast Guard, 28, 39
college placement services, 70
combination resumes, 107–111
commissions, 167
communication skills, 67,
    140–141, 146–149
communications and informa-
    tion management jobs, 110
community involvement, 78
comparison, salaries, 160–163
compensation. See benefits and
    compensation
computer skills, 67, 78
conclusions on cover letters,
    128–129
contacts
    job offers, 157–158
    networking, 83–85
    references, 77, 84
Continued Health Care Benefit
    Program (CHCBP), 39
contract resumes, 112–117

cost of living, 35, 161–162
counseling, 2, 14
    Transition Assistance
        Office, 27–28
cover letters, 125
    addressees, 127
    conclusion, 128–129
    datelines, 127
    fonts, 137–138
    format, 138
    headings, 126
    introduction, 128
    letter resumes, 135–136
    main body, 128
    networking letters,
        133–134
    paper, 138
    salutations, 127
    sample, 129
    signature block, 130
    thank-you letters, 130–132
Credentialing Opportunities
    On-Line (COOL), 61
credit ratings, 43–44
culture shock, 6–7
curriculum vitae, 118–119

D

datelines on cover letters, 127
decision-making skills, 67
Defense, Department of,
    Transportal Web site, 28
denial, 7
dental exams/insurance, 23, 40,
    168–169
depression, 7
disabled veterans, 45–46,
    55–56
discharge, 3, 11, 48
Do-It-Yourself move, 36

E

e-mailing resumes, 124

education
  benefits, 19–20
  resumes, 120
  training, 38–39, 60–61,
    72–73, 169, 181
  transcripts, 38
employers
  questions for interviewees,
    146–149
  research, 145–146,
    181–182
employment agencies, 71
employment assistance, 33–34,
  57
employment interviews, 140
entrepreneurship, 61–62
evaluation, job offers, 158–161
executive search firms, 70
expectations during job searches,
  86
expense accounts, 167
experience, 73–76, 120–121

F

family and spouse issues
  benefits, 58–59
  civilian jobs, 179–180
  coping issues, 5, 7
  federal employment,
    182–183
  job interviews, 156
  preseparation meetings, 15
  stress management, 32–33
  Web sites, 182
faxing resumes, 124
federal job listings, 82
Federal Resume Guidebook,
  121
federal resumes, 119–120
final out-processing, 49–50
financial planning, 17, 41–44,
  167
flexible work schedules, 170

follow-up phone calls after interviews, 155–156
fonts, 124, 137–138
food service jobs, 111
foreign-language skills, 78
formats for cover letters and
  resumes, 124, 138
401(k) savings, 169
functional skills, 79
funeral/bereavement, 168

G

goals/objectives, 9–11, 65–66
gossip in the office, 175
government agencies, 183
grief/mourning, 7
grooming/appearance, 16,
  142–143, 153

H

headings on cover letters and
  resumes, 91–94, 126
health care
  benefits, 57–58
  dental exams, 23
  insurance, 39–41, 168–169
  physical exams, 21, 40
  preseparation, 20
  records, copying, 25, 40
  Web sites, 183
hiring timelines, 154
hobbies/interests, 78
home loan benefits, 54–55
homeless veterans' programs,
  59
household items, 22, 35–36
housing, 6, 36

I

identification cards, 26
identity theft, 44
individualized transition plan,
  46–47

industry job directories, 82

illegal questions during an interview, 149–150

informational interviews, 139–140

insurance, health/life, 39–41, 168–169

interests/hobbies, 78

interviewing for jobs. *See also* job search
asking for a job, 154
attitude, 143–144
body language, 153–154
communication skills, 140–141
employer questions for interviewees, 146–149
employment interviews, 140
follow-up phone calls, 155–156
illegal questions, 149–150
informational interviews, 139–140
note-taking, 154
pre-interview suggestions, 141–142
punctuality, 152
questions for the employer, 150–151
screening interviews, 140
thank-you notes, 156

introductions on cover letters, 128

J

jargon, military, 97–100

job fairs, 16, 82

job hunting, 4

job offer initial evaluation checklist, 159

job search. *See also* interviewing for jobs
advertisements, 1, 81–83

attitude, 86

civilian jobs, 176–177, 183

education and training, 52–53

evaluation of job offers, 158–161

employment assistance, 33–34

employment interviews, 140

expectations, 86

family and spouse issues, 87

job offers, 157–158

myths and realities, 64–65

organizational skills, 67–68

research, 14, 17

salaries, 43, 150, 162

sales pitch, 86

skills, updating, 177

Web sites, 34, 183

jury duty, 168

K–L

knowledge, skills, and abilities (KSAs), 121

Labor, U.S. Department of, 70, 163

legal issues
job offers, 158
jury duty, 168

legislative agencies, 183

length of resumes, 124

letter resumes, 135–136

licensing and certification, 38, 60–61, 121

life insurance, 39–41, 53–54, 169

life values, 80–81

listening skills, 154

local job listings, 82

M

main body of cover letters, 128

management, supervision, and administration jobs, 110
Marine Corps, 28, 38
marketable skills, 78
master career catalog checklist, 72–78
medical issues. *See* health care
memberships, 78
military
    associations, 183
    components, 185–186
    jargon, 97–100
    records, 48
mistakes on the job, 177
Montgomery GI Bill, 37
mortgage insurance, 54
mourning/grief, 7
myths and realities about job search, 64–65

N

National Defense Authorization Act, 55
Native Americans, 55
Navy
    education transcripts, 38
    Transition Assistance Office, 28
negotiation for salaries, 163–166
networking
    contact list, 77, 83–85
    civilian jobs, 22, 24, 173–174
    letters, 133–134
    office gossip, 175
    preseparation, 16
    support groups, 7
news services, 184
note-taking during interviews, 154

O

O*NET OnLine Web site, 111
objectives/goals, 65–66, 91, 94

Occupational Outlook Handbook, 163
offers for jobs, 157
office administration jobs, 110
office gossip, 175
on-the-job skills, 177
online calculators, 35
organizational skills during job search, 67–68
out-processing, 49–50
outplacement specialists, 3
overseas benefits/employment, 15, 59

P

paid time off, 168–170
paper for cover letters and resumes, 138
paperwork, 4–6
peers in the military, 5
pension, disability, 56–57
performance bonuses, 167
perks. *See* benefits and compensation
permissive travel, 36
personal days, 168
personal information, 72, 119
personal pronouns on resumes, 123
personnel records, 15
physical exams, 21, 40
power words on resumes, 103, 123
pre-interview suggestions, 141–142
preseparation
    counseling checklist (DD 2648), 29–31
    stress management, 17, 32–33
    timeline activities checklist, 13–26
professional organizations, 78, 169

professional references, 77, 84
proofreading resumes, 122–123
psychological issues, 7
punctuality for interviews, 152

Q–R

qualifications summaries on
  resumes, 91, 95–96
questions during interviews,
  146–151
realistic expectations during job
  search, 86
realities and myths about job
  search, 64–65
records, military, 48
references, 77, 84
reinstatement eligibility for
  federal jobs, 120
relocation assistance, 19, 24,
  34–37, 167, 171, 184
researching employers, 145–146,
  181–182
reserves, 18, 45, 168
resumes
  capitalization, 123
  chronological, 104–106
  combination, 107–111
  contract, 112–117
  curriculum vitae, 118–119
  e-mailing, 124
  faxing, 124
  federal, 119–120
  fonts, 124, 137–138
  formats, 124
  headings, 91–94
  knowledge, skills, and
    abilities (KSAs), 121
  length, 124
  letter resumes, 135–136
  military jargon, 97–100
  objectives, 91, 94
  paper, 138
  personal pronouns, 123

preseparation, 18
power words, 103, 123
proofreading, 89–90,
  122–123
punctuation, 123–124
qualifications summary,
  91, 95–96
salary history/
  requirements, 122
sentence structure,
  102–103
spell-checking, 123
updating, 123, 177–178
verb tense, 123
Web sites, 121
retirement
  benefits, 47
  listening, 154
  preparation, 10–11
  veterans and retirees, 185

S

salaries
  comparison, 150, 160–163
  negotiation, 43, 163–166
  resumes, 122
sales and training jobs, 111
sales pitch during job search, 86
salutations on cover letters,
  127–128
savings, 41
screening interviews, 140
self-employment, 61, 184
self-management skills, 80
sentence structure on resumes,
  102–103
separation pay, 41–42
service agencies, 185
Service-Disabled Veterans'
  Insurance (RH Insurance), 54
Servicemembers' Group Life
  Insurance (SGLI), 26, 39,
  53–54

setting goals/objectives, 65–66
severance package, 170
shipping household items, 35–36
sick days, 168
sign-on bonuses, 167
signature blocks on cover letters, 130
skills
    assessments, 15, 38
    communication, 67, 140–141, 146–149
    computer, 67, 78
    decision-making, 67
    foreign languages, 78
    marketable, 78
    self-management, 80
    technical, 79
    transferable/functional, 79
    updating, 177
Small Business Administration, 61
Special Separation Benefits (SSB), 56
spell-checking, 123
spouse and family
    civilian jobs, 179–180
    coping issues, 5, 7
    job interviews/searches, 87, 156
    preseparation meetings, 15
    stress management, 32–33
    Web sites, 182
Standardized Installation Topic Exchange System (SITES), 34–35
states
    benefits, 59–60
    job listings, 82
    veterans' homes, 59
stock options, 169
storage of household items, 22, 35–36

stress management, 3, 7
    job offers, 157
    preseparation, 17, 32–33
support groups, 7
survivor benefits, 58–59

T

tax assistance, 167
technical, mechanical, and construction jobs, 111
technical skills, 79
telecommuting, 170
testing services, 38
thank-you letters, 130–132, 155
Thrift Savings Plan, 41
timelines
    employment hiring, 154
    job searches, 68
    transition, 9–11, 13–26
training, on-the-job skills, 38–39, 169, 177
transcripts, education, 38
transferable skills, 79
Transition Assistance Office, 2, 4, 7, 27–28
    employment assistance, 33–34, 70
    preseparation checklist, 13–26
transition issues
    timelines, 9–11
    Web sites, 184
transportation/logistics jobs, 111
typefaces for cover letters and resumes, 137–138

U–V

unemployment compensation benefits, 25, 42
university placement services, 70
updating
    job skills, 177
    resumes, 123, 177–178

Use Your Military Experience & Training (UMET), 60
vacation days, 168
values, life/work, 80–81
verb tense on resumes, 123
Verification of Military Experience and Training (DD Form 2586), 18, 22, 34
Veterans Administration Web site, 51
Veterans Affairs Disability Application Form (21-526), 26
veterans and retirees, 185
    benefits, 24, 47
    disabled, 45–46
Veterans Educational Assistance Program (VEAP), 37
Veterans' Application for Compensation or Pension Form (21–526), 56
Veterans' Group Life Insurance (VGLI), 26, 39–40, 54
Veterans' Mortgage Life Insurance (VMLI), 54
Veterans' Preference, 119–120
vision insurance, 168–169
vocation rehabilitation, 56–57
Volunteer Separation Incentives (VSI), 56
voter information, 185

W–Z

wardrobe, civilian, 16, 21, 142–143, 153
Web sites
    career decision making, 181
    civilian jobs, 183
    compensation and benefits, 184

credit ratings, 43–44
    Department of Defense, 28, 34
    education, 181
    employer research, 181–182
    family and spouse issues, 182
    federal employment, 182
    government agencies, 183
    health care, 183
    international military bases, 34–35
    job listings, 82
    legislative agencies, 183
    military associations, 183–184
    military components, 185–186
    news services, 184
    O*NET OnLine, 101
    online calculators, 35
    relocation assistance, 184
    The Resume Place, 182
    resumes, 121
    salaries, 163
    self-employment, 184–185
    service agencies, 185
    transition, 184
    Veterans Administration, 51
    veterans and retirees, 37, 43, 185
    voter information, 185
work experience, 73–76, 120–121
work values, 80–81
Workforce Investment Act, 37, 60